THE ROLE OF STATE SUPREME COURTS IN THE NEW JUDICIAL FEDERALISM

Recent Titles in Contributions in Legal Studies
Series Editor: Paul L. Murphy

Prologue to Nuremberg: The Politics and Diplomacy of Punishing War Criminals of the First World War
James F. Willis

The Network of Control: State Supreme Courts and State Security Statutes, 1920–1970
Carol E. Jenson

Drugs and Information Control: The Role of Men and Manipulation in the Control of Drug Trafficking
Jerald W. Cloyd

State Supreme Courts: Policymakers in the Federal System
Mary Cornelia Porter and G. Alan Tarr, editors

The Future of Our Liberties: Perspectives on the Bill of Rights
Stephen C. Halpern, editor

Tightening the Reins of Justice in America: A Comparative Analysis of the Criminal Jury Trial in England and the United States
Michael H. Graham

The Development of Law on the Rocky Mountain Frontier: Civil Law and Society, 1850–1912
Gordon Morris Bakken

Clients and Lawyers: Securing the Rights of Disabled Persons
Susan M. Olson

The New High Priests: Lawyers in Post-Civil War America
Gerard W. Gawalt, editor

The Little Rock Crisis: A Constitutional Interpretation
Tony Freyer

Nuclear Weapons and Law
Arthur Selwyn Miller and Martin Feinrider, editors

Native American Aliens: Disloyalty and the Renunciation of Citizenship by Japanese Americans during World War II
Donald E. Collins

Corwin's Constitution: Essays and Insights of Edward S. Corwin
Kenneth D. Crews, editor

The Role of State Supreme Courts in the New Judicial Federalism

———————— SUSAN P. FINO

CONTRIBUTIONS IN LEGAL STUDIES, NUMBER 36

GREENWOOD PRESS

NEW YORK
WESTPORT, CONNECTICUT
LONDON

Library of Congress Cataloging-in-Publication Data

Fino, Susan P., 1954–
  The role of state supreme courts in the new judicial federalism.
  (Contributions in legal studies, ISSN 0147-1074 ; no. 36)
  Bibliography: p.
  Includes index.
  1. Courts of last resort—United States—States.
  2. United States—Constitutional law, State. I. Title.
  II. Series.
  KF8736.F56   1987   347.73'36   86-19439
                         347.30735
  ISBN 0-313-25437-0 (lib. bdg. : alk. paper)

Copyright © 1987 by Susan P. Fino

All rights reserved. No portion of this book may be reproduced, by any process or technique, without the express written consent of the publisher.

Library of Congress Catalog Card Number: 86-19439
ISBN: 0-313-25437-0
ISSN: 0147-1074

347.7336
F515r

First published in 1987

Greenwood Press, Inc.
88 Post Road West, Westport, Connecticut 06881

Printed in the United States of America

The paper used in this book complies with the Permanent Paper Standard issued by the National Information Standards Organization (Z39.48-1984).

10 9 8 7 6 5 4 3 2 1

For my family

Contents

Figures and Tables	ix
Preface	xi
1. A Model of Supreme Court Performance	1
2. Institutional Characteristics of State Supreme Courts	25
3. The Justices	49
4. The Work of Six Supreme Courts	65
5. A Closer Look at Six Courts	87
6. Conclusions	111
Appendix	119
Bibliography	143
Index to Cases	147
Subject Index	149

Figures and Tables

FIGURES

1.1	Some Factors Related to State Supreme Court Performance	7
4.1	Issues in Six State Supreme Courts, 1975	69
5.1	Issues in Arizona Supreme Court, 1975	88
5.2	Issues in Arizona Supreme Court, 1975 (Panel Cases Only)	90
5.3	Issues in California Supreme Court, 1975	92
5.4	Issues in Kentucky Court of Appeals, 1975	95
5.5	Issues in Michigan Supreme Court, 1975	98
5.6	Issues in Nebraska Supreme Court, 1975	101
5.7	Issues in Nebraska Supreme Court, 1975 (Panel Cases Only)	104
5.8	Issues in New Jersey Supreme Court, 1975	106

TABLES

1.1	Political Culture and Expected Features of the State Judiciary	12
2.1	Term of Office, Courts of Last Resort, 1976, 1978	27
2.2	Formal Judicial Recruitment in the States, 1976, 1978	29

2.3	Variations in Institutional Characteristics, 1976, 1978	30
2.4	Staffing the State Courts, 1976, 1978	32
2.5	Regional Variations in Formal Judicial Recruitment, 1976	33
2.6	Regional Variations in Formal Judicial Recruitment, 1978	33
2.7	Regional Variations in Judicial Selection and Supervision, 1976, 1978	36
2.8	The 1976 Court Classes: Method of Selection	44
2.9	The 1978 Court Classes: Method of Selection	45
3.1	All Justices: State Courts of Last Resort, 1975, 1977	52
4.1	All En Banc Cases	72
A.1	Factor Loadings: Rotated Factor Matrix, 1976, 1978	121
A.2	Formal Recruitment and Judicial Backgrounds, 1975, 1977	122
A.3	Regional Variations in Judicial Backgrounds, 1975, 1977	126
A.4	Comparing Interim Appointees and Formally Recruited Justices, 1975, 1977	130
A.5	Classification of State Supreme Court Cases	134
A.6	En Banc State Statutory Cases	138
A.7	En Banc Common-Law Cases	139
A.8	En Banc Criminal Cases	140
A.9	En Banc Criminal Constitutional Cases	141
A.10	En Banc Constitutional Cases	142

Preface

Legal scholars and political scientists recently have "rediscovered" state constitutions and state supreme courts. In the last several years, numerous articles have appeared in the law reviews investigating the role of state courts of last resort in the development of state constitutional law, especially in the areas of civil rights and liberties. Whether this new interest in state courts is the product of a conservative's "new federalism" or a liberal's search for alternatives to the Burger Court is open to debate. Whatever the reasons for the reconsideration of state courts and state law, as a political scientist, I welcome the opportunity to study state supreme courts in the larger context of American federalism.

This book represents an initial effort to lay the foundation for the systematic study of state supreme courts and their performance, especially in the area of the development of an independent and adequate body of state constitutional law. I integrate the findings of a number of social scientists into a comprehensive model of state supreme court performance and test the utility of the model in an investigation of the institutional structure of state court systems, the social backgrounds of the justices and the docket of six selected state courts. The reader will find that, on occasion, I illustrate my arguments with some quantitative findings. However, even those who winced when the grammar-school teacher reached for the flashcards need not worry about what little "math" appears in this book. For the most part, simple percentage comparisons are the only statistical techniques used. However, even this rather elementary quantitative technique creates a broader and more accurate picture of the state courts, their justices and their decisions than would be possible by the more traditional case analysis. My study of state supreme courts focuses on the years 1975 and 1977. These years were not chosen arbitrarily; rather they represent the beginning of the interest in the new judicial federalism. Probably, much has changed since these early years, but the model of performance and the findings for the six courts featured in this study can form a valuable baseline for future work.

I should point out a number of biases and assumptions present here. I begin with the assumption that courts in America can and do make policy. It is too late in the day to argue that judges simply serve as living oracles of the law. Therefore, the appropriate area of study for a social scientist is not whether or not judges make law, but how they do it, how well they do it and when they should do it. I am also a supporter of the development of an independent body of state constitutional law for the protection of individual rights. I agree with Justice William Brennan that one of the geniuses of the American federal system is the allowance for the double protection of individual rights made possible by the presence of the federal and state constitutions.

I am grateful to a number of individuals for their assistance with this book. Professors Robert Alexander, Ross K. Baker, Milton Heumann and Jay Sigler offered valuable insights and criticisms. Keith Denny performed the unenviable task of checking my sources and quotations and tracking down the parallel cites to the cases. Nancy Kaminski helped type the manuscript, and Lisa Greifenberg, Brian T. Levine and Joann Condino prepared the tables and figures. Kraig Binkowski did a most able job as the graphic artist, and Kai Christensen exterminated the bugs in my computer files. Most of all, however, I need to thank Professor Stanley H. Friedelbaum, who not only reviewed my work with the greatest care, but also introduced me to this most fascinating area of study.

THE ROLE OF STATE SUPREME COURTS IN THE NEW JUDICIAL FEDERALISM

1. A Model of Supreme Court Performance

For many years, scholars in the field of public law have focused almost exclusively on the United States Supreme Court as the best example of judicial policymaking. The Court's activities have been studied as the products of the doctrinal development of the case law, the interaction of small groups, the formation of voting blocs and as a function of the social backgrounds and attitudes of the individual justices.[1] With the universal acceptance of the Court's role as a maker of public policy, specific court decisions have been analyzed and criticized in terms of their outcomes and impacts.[2] Now a Supreme Court decision is no longer evaluated as simply "good law" or "bad law"; it is examined also as good or bad social policy.[3]

There are undoubtedly many reasons for political scientists to have concentrated heavily on the United States Supreme Court. One of the most obvious and prosaic reasons is the ease of data collection and analysis. There have been only approximately one hundred justices ever appointed to the Court, and their judicial biographies are commonly available. The decisions of the Court, published in three forms, are readily accessible in any major library. However, there are more important reasons for concentrating on the United States Supreme Court. The Court is a national body—one of three co-equal branches of the federal government—and, therefore, its decisions often have widespread and dramatic impact on public policy. Moreover, for a long time the Court itself may have discouraged the study of state courts' roles in the creation of public policy. The Roosevelt Court was responsible for the interment of the Tenth Amendment as a "truism" in *United States v. Darby*, 312 U.S. 100, 61 S.Ct. 451, 85 L.Ed.

609 (1941), and the Warren Court has "nationalized" virtually the entire Bill of Rights.[4] Over a quarter century of emphasis on the federal role in the protection of federal rights and liberties, combined with the disrepute state courts fell into during the era of desegregation, make it easy to understand how state courts have come to be neglected and their impact on public policy ignored.

However, new interest in the states and state supreme courts has developed in the last ten years, an interest which has been sparked by two very different sources: the liberal and conservative factions of the United States Supreme Court.

Chief Justice Warren Burger and Justice William Rehnquist, who represent the conservative point of view, seem concerned with the integrity of the states in our federal system for both philosophical and pragmatic reasons. Justice Rehnquist has sought to curb federal interference in state affairs in an effort to maintain the states as the functional units of government. His plurality opinion in *National League of Cities v. Usery*, 426 U.S. 833, 96 S. Ct. 2465, 49 L.Ed.2d 245 (1976), attempted to resurrect the Tenth Amendment as a barrier to federal intrusion in areas he deems essential to the states' functioning as states.[5] The Chief Justice also has urged that the states, and especially state courts, be taken seriously but for a different reason. For Chief Justice Burger, state supreme courts are an ideal mechanism by which the caseload of the United States Supreme Court can be reduced without resorting to a greatly expanded lower federal judiciary or the unpopular idea of a national court of appeals. Of course, state supreme courts can serve as such a mechanism only if they are equal with federal courts in their ability to adjudicate constitutional claims. Also, the conservative majority of the Court seems to assume that such parity exists, as illustrated by the decision in *Stone v. Powell*, 428 U.S. 465, 96 S.Ct. 3037, 49 L.Ed.2d 1067 (1975).[6]

Justice William Brennan, perhaps the most liberal member of the Supreme Court, believes that fellow liberals with constitutional claims should consider seeking redress in state supreme courts in light of the Burger Court's recent retrenchments in the areas of equal protection, due process and criminal justice. Justice Brennan sees state constitutions as "fonts of individual liberties, their protections often extending beyond those required by the Supreme Court's interpretation of federal law" (1977: 91). He urges the consideration of state constitutional analogs to the Bill of Rights and the use of independent and adequate grounds to shield decisions from the federal court's review. For Justice Brennan, the strength of our federal system lies in the "double protection" afforded individual rights and liberties by the presence of the national and state constitutions. Apparently having no trouble with the argument for national standards for fundamental rights, Justice Brennan cites with approval the civil libertarian decisions of the California and New Jersey supreme courts. Liberals, then, see state courts and state constitutions as means to avoid the conservative outcomes of decisions by the United States Supreme Court.

While Chief Justice Burger may believe that state courts of last resort are the functional equivalents of federal courts in their ability to adjudicate constitutional claims, others are not so certain. Professor Burt Neuborne (1977) has urged the expansion of the federal judiciary so that civil libertarians will be able to avoid state courts and secure prompt, favorable outcomes in federal courts. He argues that the federal courts are better equipped to decide complex constitutional questions which often involve the balancing of competing, legitimate interests. He is careful to cite certain institutional differences between federal and state courts which he asserts make the federal courts better decision-makers than their state counterparts: the relatively small size of the federal bench; the independence of judges resulting from life tenure; higher salaries (which recruit better legal talent) and better technical and clerical support for legal research. However, Neuborne is unable to provide any data to support his assertions, and, more importantly, he seems to assume all state courts are alike. They are not: state courts vary from the grossly underpaid and poorly assisted courts of Mississippi and Utah to the well-provided-for courts of New York, New Jersey and California. Yet so far no one has assessed the institutional features of state supreme courts to determine which courts, if any, can serve as the functional equivalents of federal courts.

This new reliance upon state courts of last resort creates a need for answers to questions concerning the ability of state courts to play an enhanced role in complicated, policy-oriented litigation. Since there are fifty different state court systems, we need to develop a conceptual and operational definition of a "good" state supreme court so that we may identify courts already capable of serving as functional equivalents of the federal courts and see areas of improvement for those which are not. We then need to discover what particular features of state court systems are not only associated with "good" performance but, for practical purposes, are capable of being changed. The purpose of this book is threefold:

1. to propose a conceptual and operational definition of a "good" state supreme court
2. to integrate various findings from the literature into a comprehensive, theoretical model to help explain some factors related to state supreme court performance
3. to suggest the utility of the definition and model through the examination of the institutional features of the fifty state court systems; the social backgrounds of state court of last resort justices and the decisions of selected state supreme courts

This book focuses on state courts of last resort, but these courts will be treated in the context of the entire state judicial system. There are two justifications for this approach. First, the bulk of any state supreme court's jurisdiction is appellate; therefore, the issues and facts reaching the highest court will be framed in the courts below. Second, state courts of last resort are charged with two distinct responsibilities. The usual focus of research is the responsibility of these courts to function as appellate decision-makers, correcting the legal errors of and formulating broad legal rules for the courts below. However, state supreme courts also are responsible for the administration of the state bar and the lower state judiciary. Because the amount of judicial time and energy is finite, the more time spent discharging one responsibility, the less time available for the other. Problems in the administration of the bar and the lower courts will divert time and energy from the total amount available for the consideration of appellate cases. Therefore, the quality and efficiency of the lower courts are inextricably linked to state supreme court performance.

AN INDICATOR OF STATE SUPREME COURT PERFORMANCE

Any conceptual definition of a "good" state supreme court must take into account three factors. First, the definition must incorporate the unique role of state courts in the development and interpretation of state law. Next, any conceptual or operational definition must avoid the pitfall of equating the proportion of constitutional decisions by a state supreme court with judicial activism. Such an equation ignores the potential for the creative uses of statutory interpretation or the common law and fails to distinguish between the federal standards required by the federal Constitution and the independent standards available under the state constitution. Finally, a conceptual definition, as far as possible, should not be ideologically charged. A given state supreme court's performance should not be assessed as "good" simply because its decisions are in agreement with the ideological predilections of the researcher. For example, a court should not be rated favorably because its opinions reflect the appropriate proportions of "pro-criminal defendant," "pro-civil liberties" or "pro-economic underdog" decisions.

Keeping in mind these three factors, along with the belief that the states are important functional units in the American federal system, I propose the following conceptual definition: a "good" state supreme court is one which is committed to the development of an independent body of state law through the rendition of principled decisions. Here, principled decisions are those based upon more than personal whim or exigent circumstances; instead, principled decisions embody historical and legal considerations which help to make the law knowable. Once this definition is accepted, the task is to "operationalize" it so that state supreme court performance can be assessed quantitatively. By this definition, a "good" state supreme court is also an "activist" supreme court in the development of state law.

Mary Cornelia Porter (1978) has suggested criteria for evaluating state supreme court activism, and some of her standards can be adapted to help operationalize the definition of a good court. She believes that an activist court is one which is committed to the construction of the state constitution, provides leadership for other states and is sensitive to the importance of judicial craftsmanship to lend legitimacy to its opinions. These criteria suggest that an activist court can be identified by looking for the following elements in its opinions: (1) the reliance on independent and adequate state grounds; (2) the citation of precedents borrowed from sister states and (3) the citation of law review or other scholarly articles. The use of independent and adequate state grounds—legal arguments which rest exclusively on state law and, therefore, preclude review by federal courts—demonstrates the commitment to the development of state law. The citation of sister state precedents, as well as law review articles or other materials, captures both the ideas of leadership and craftsmanship. These citations also help to give quantitative meaning to the notion of a principled opinion.

The three elements of judicial activism can be combined into an indicator of state supreme court performance. This indicator avoids the problems of value-laden indices and indices equating performance with constitutional decisions while capturing the importance of the development of state law via principled opinions. The indicator also has several practical features. It is easy to code state supreme court decisions operationalized in this manner. Sister state precedents and law review citations can be counted, and this procedure involves no judgment calls on the part of the researcher. The use of independent and adequate state grounds is a bit more problematic because of the degree of uncertainty in establishing just exactly what constitutes an independent and adequate state ground. However, I believe the problem can be minimized through the creation of narrow decision-rules for the coding of an opinion. An example of such decision-rules is contained in the methodology section of Chapter 4. Because of the ease in coding, minimal training is needed for coders, and a large number of cases can be coded in a relatively short period of time. More importantly, I believe this indicator is highly reliable because only one element is dependent on the judgment of the coder. Throughout the remainder of this book, this indicator will serve as one of a number of dependent variables.

A MODEL OF STATE SUPREME COURT PERFORMANCE

Figure 1.1 represents a model of some factors related to state supreme court performance. The model is the result of the integration of the findings of numerous researchers on the states and the state courts. For convenience in discussion, the paths in the model have been labeled with letters or letters with numerals, and the names of the researchers who have suggested the relationships appear associated with the appropriate arrows.

Path A represents the relationship between state socioeconomic diversity and what Daniel J. Elazar (1966) has called "political culture." For Elazar, a state's social and economic diversity will affect the degree of internal unity of the state and the general relationship between

Figure 1.1 Some Factors Related to State Supreme Court Performance

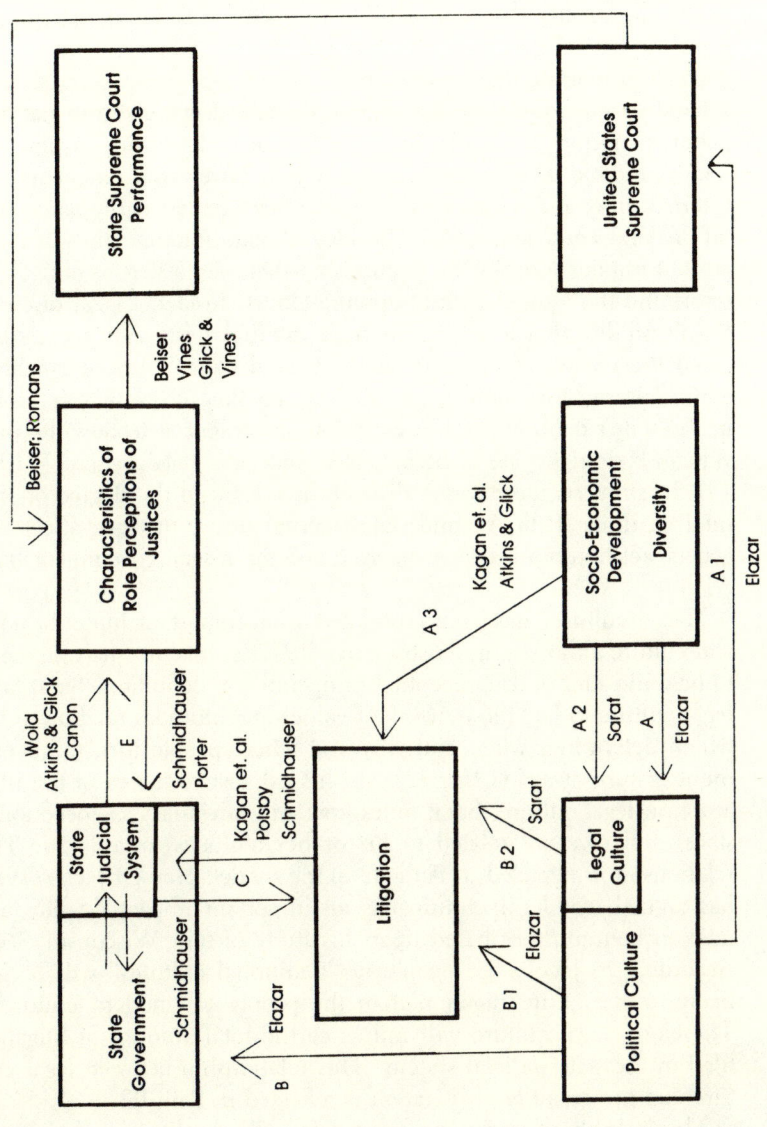

the state and the federal government: the greater the degree of internal unity, the greater the state's ability to resist "outside encroachment" from the federal government. State internal unity is a function of the degree of intrastate sharing of patterns, norms and policy interests considered in relationship to the degree of state deviation from national patterns, norms and policy interests. These relationships suggest that socioeconomic diversity within a state will have an adverse effect on internal unity and, consequently, make the state less equipped to fend off "federal encroachment." The idea of state internal unity has important implications for the relationships between a state's court of last resort and the United States Supreme Court. In fact, Elazar discusses the possibility that a state with high internal unity can successfully avoid the impact of decisions of the federal Court "if they can bring courts, prosecutors, police, and the bar together at the state level and in the state's communities in common agreement as to how the individual's basic rights are to be protected under the state's scheme" (1966: 13). In sum, socioeconomic diversity is related to the degree of state internal unity (Path A), and state internal unity, in turn, affects the general relationship between the state and the federal government (Path A1).

"Legal culture" has been postulated as an important subset of political culture although, as Austin Sarat (1977) points out, no one seems to be quite sure of its conceptual or operational definition. Sarat takes legal culture to be "the network of values and attitudes relating to law which determines when and why and where people turn to government or turn away" (1977: 427). In his exhaustive survey of the literature on legal culture, Sarat notes how an individual's socioeconomic status and race are related to his or her attitudes toward law. This relationship is depicted in Path A2 of the model. Herbert Jacob (1980) has argued that legal culture has an important impact on litigation rates in communities based upon his study of four Wisconsin cities. According to Jacob, the people of "traditional cultures" will be less likely to engage in litigation than the people of "modern cultures." Therefore, legal culture will influence the total amount of litigation filed in the state judicial system. This relationship between legal culture and the quantity of litigation is reflected in Path B2.

The quantity of litigation in the states will also be related to socioeconomic development and socioeconomic diversity as indicated by Path A3. In a study of sixteen state supreme courts in sixteen sample years, Robert A. Kagan, Bliss Cartwright, Lawrence M. Friedman and Stanton Wheeler (1978) found that increased population was associated with an increased caseload for the state supreme court. The increased demand on the courts usually prompted institutional reform of the state judiciary, which frequently took the form of the creation of an intermediate appellate court (Path C). Burton M. Atkins and Henry R. Glick (1976) studied the effect of environmental and structural variables on the issues appearing in a state's supreme court. They found that the supreme courts of rural and politically undifferentiated states tended to handle a relatively high proportion of private litigation, while the courts of states scoring high on affluence, economic development and political professionalism more frequently rendered decisions concerning civil liberties and economic regulation. Thus, the nature of the issues, the quality of cases appearing in state courts as well as the quantity of cases is related to socioeconomic conditions within a state, as reflected in Path A3.

For Elazar, political culture is one of three "overarching factors . . . especially important in shaping the individual states' political structures, electoral behavior and modes of organization for political action" (1966: 79).[7] There are three political cultures which are particularly important in shaping the operation of the state political system within the context of American federalism:

They are (1) the set of perception of what politics is and what can be expected from government held by both the general public and the politicians; (2) the kinds of people who become active in government and politics, as holders of elective offices, members of the bureaucracy and active political workers; and (3) the active way in which the art of government is practiced by citizens, politicians and public officials in light of their perceptions. (1966: 84–85)

If Elazar is correct, then we should expect the political cultures of the individual states to set the boundaries for political behavior and help determine the form government institutions will take and the kinds of individuals who will fill public office. This relationship is shown in Path B. I also would suggest that political culture not only helps shape the practice of politics in the state but also helps determine the kinds of cases filed in state courts. Therefore, I have included Path B1 in the model.

The political culture of a particular state embodies both elements of

American political culture—the concept of the marketplace, the idea of bargaining and rational self-interest; and the concept of commonwealth, the ideal of community interest in the best government to implement shared moral principles—to varying degrees. In the Individualistic or "I" culture, the emphasis is on marketplace values, the triumph of private concerns over community interests. The "I" culture resembles the contract societies of Thomas Hobbes and John Locke. Politics is perceived as another form of professional business activity; it is essentially "a dirty business left to those who choose to pursue it." However, since these politicians are professional people, they should be amply rewarded for their expertise. Therefore, in "I" cultures, I would expect to find career judges who are well salaried for their efforts. Like an ideal market system, the Individualistic culture should feature competitive party politics; consequently, I would expect to find judicial selection via partisan election in these states. Efficiency is also a market value, and I would expect this value to be reflected in a highly bureaucratized state court system. Finally, since the pure Individualistic culture is devoid of community interests, the role of government is to serve as referee among many competing individual interests, not to implement any broad policy of the public good. Therefore, I believe that, in general, litigation rates in "I" cultures will be relatively high, and I would expect to find challenges to economic regulation as well as a good deal of private litigation in the courts.

Unlike the Individualistic political culture, the Moralistic or "M" culture emphasizes the commonwealth—the ideal of a common good and a public interest. This culture is more of the kind of civic society envisioned by Jean-Jacques Rousseau. Government is not left to the professional politician; instead it is the duty of every citizen. Consequently, I would expect to see fewer career judges on the courts of Moralistic states and lower judicial salaries. There is little tolerance of corruption in these states, and political party regularity is not important. Given these considerations, I would expect judicial selection via merit plan or nonpartisan election and a litany of formal qualifications for judges and justices written into state law. Government intervention is expected for the sake of the public good in a Moralistic culture. Therefore, I would not anticipate challenges to the scope of government regulation in the courts. Instead, there will be challenges to the nature of regulation because the conception of what is necessary to the public good will change from era to era. Finally, I would expect to

A Model of Supreme Court Performance							11

see a relatively large fraction of criminal cases and a relatively small fraction of cases concerning individual rights in states dominated by the Moralistic political culture.

The third political culture—the Traditionalistic or "T"—features "ambivalent attitudes towards the marketplace combined with a paternalistic and elitist conception of the commonwealth" (Elazar, 1966: 93). The Traditionalistic culture embodies a Burkean view of society: human society is hierarchical as part of the ordered nature of the universe, and the appropriate role for the government is the maintenance of hierarchy rather than the imposition of equality. Elazar points out that Traditionalistic cultures "confine real political power to a relatively small and self-perpetuating group drawn from an established elite" (1966: 93). This culture is "instinctively antibureaucratic" because "by its very nature bureaucracy interferes with the fine web of informal personal relationships that lie at the root of the political system" (1966: 94). This description of the Traditionalistic political culture leads me to a number of expectations about litigation and the structure of the judiciary in these states. I would expect most judges and justices to come from old, well-established families with long-standing social and political connections. I would expect to find antique and inefficient institutions because of hostility to bureaucracy and resistance to reform. Litigation rates in Traditionalistic cultures probably would be quite low: disputes among the elites would be resolved informally while disputes between elites and lower classes, especially those involving equal protection, would be taken to federal court. Finally, given the emphasis on the maintenance of the established order, I believe courts in traditionalistic states will settle a good deal of disputes concerning property and the common law guided by the principle of *stare decisis*.

Political culture is often treated as a residual category, like Alzheimer's disease. When all other sources of variation in behavior have been ruled out, the residuum is labeled "political culture." However, I believe that through a careful analysis of the elements of each type of political culture, political culture can be elevated from residual category to independent variable. The relationship between political culture and state judicial systems is indicated in Paths B and B1 of the model, and my expectations concerning this relationship are summarized in Table 1.1.

A state judicial system does not exist in isolation: it is but one institution within a tripartite system of government (Path D). The judici-

Table 1.1 Political Culture and Expected Features of the State Judiciary

POLITICAL CULTURE	RELATIVE LITIGATION RATE	LITIGATION TYPES	PROBABLE INSTITUTIONAL FEATURES OF STATE JUDICIARY	ADDITIONAL EXPECTATIONS
Individualistic	High	-private economic (e.g. contracts) -challenges to scope of government intervention (especially in economic affairs) -individual rights and liberties	-highly paid, career judiciary -judicial selection on a partisan basis (partisan or legislative election, gubernatorial appointment without "merit" lists) -large court system -highly bureaucratized court system	-high dissent rates
Moralistic	Moderate	-challenges to nature of government intervention -criminal cases	-judicial selection by merit system or non-partisan elections -judicial commission or courts on the judicial to lessen chance of corruption -low salaries	-low dissent rates
Traditionalistic	Low	-few civil liberties (esp. equal protection)	-judiciary of local elites -antiquated system of courts	-low dissent rates -rule of <u>stare decisis</u>

ary, because it holds neither the power of the purse nor the power of the sword, is dependent on the state legislature and state executive. However, the appropriate degree of dependence for the state judiciary on other branches of government is unknown. Under the American constitutional system, the judiciary must be independent enough to determine the requirements of the rule of law but not so unrestrained as to thwart democratic government by becoming what Learned Hand has called a "bevy of Platonic Guardians." John R. Schmidhauser (1979) has proposed nine variables to assess the degree of independence of the state judiciary with respect to the other branches of government:

1. the separation of the courts from the political branches of government
2. the foundation of judicial authority: whether constitutionally established or dependent on the caprice of the legislature
3. the tenure of judges and justices
4. the irreducibility of judicial salaries
5. the selection standards for judges and justices
6. the constitutional guarantee of judicial review
7. the degree of compliance with decisions
8. the specification of clearly defined, universalistic jurisdiction for the appellate judiciary
9. the presence of regularized judicial institutional procedures and norms

I would suggest that the greater the judicial independence, as measured by any one of Schmidhauser's variables or a combination of variables in an index of judicial independence, the greater the degree of judicial activism by the state's court of last resort. Furthermore, the variations in institutional characteristics among the fifty state court systems provide an ideal mechanism by which the effect of judicial independence on state court activism may be assessed.

The institutional characteristics of the state judiciary are not only a function of the need for judicial independence within a system of checks and balances, they are also a response to the quantity of litigation in the states as depicted in Path C. Kagan et al. (1978) saw how the increase in litigation in a state's courts typically prompted the creation of an intermediate court of appeals. The work of Nelson Polsby (1968) on Congress also suggests that certain changes in an organization set in once the organization achieves a certain "critical mass" of work to be performed. Polsby labels this process "institutionalization," and he argues that this process is necessary for the survival, stability and efficient functioning of the organization. For Polsby, institutionalization consists of three elements: the establishment of boundaries which set off an organization from its environment; the development of specialized functional units within the organization and the development of standardized norms and procedures. Schmidhauser (1979) applies the concept of institutionalization to the struggle for independence of the federal judiciary from Congress and the President, and this application readily can be extended to the state judiciary.

While a certain level of institutionalization may be necessary for the survival, stability and independence of an organization, the process may have a limit at which any increased institutionalization is counterproductive. The more the internal complexity of an organization and the greater its size, the more time and energy must be devoted to the simple task of administering the organization. Such a situation becomes particularly problematic when a unit within the organization is charged with both the responsibility to administer the organization and the responsibility to perform other required tasks. This is precisely the case of a state supreme court which must supervise the bar and the lower judiciary as well as serve as appellate decision-maker. The more time and energy spent in a supervisory capacity, the less time available for the court's primary responsibility of adjudication. Therefore, the growth and specialization of a court system may quickly reach the limit at which they are counterproductive unless the system is furnished with specialized structures—court planning or judicial administration offices—to help fulfill the administrative and supervisory requirements of the system.[8] Once again, variations in the size, complexity and administration of the fifty state court systems provide an ideal comparative perspective from which the limits of institutionalization may be assessed.

The effect of institutional characteristics on state supreme court decision-making should be of special interest to social scientists and anyone else interested in court reform because these features of the court system can be changed. We cannot compel citizens to file interesting constitutional cases in state court, but we can alter the institutional structure of the state judiciary in the name of reform. Here we can draw from the wealth of materials on the bureaucracy and organizational theory.⁹

In Figure 1.1, Paths C and D have arrows drawn in both directions. Atkins and Glick (1974) have noted how certain institutional characteristics of a state court system—particularly the presence of an intermediate appellate court—are related to the nature of issues appearing in a state supreme court. The intermediate court provides a screening function for the court of last resort. Routine or trivial cases are reviewed in the intermediate appellate court so that the state supreme court is freed to handle cases with important implications for the law and public policy. Path D represents the relationship between the state judiciary and other branches of the state government. Obviously (and especially through judicial review) the state judiciary will have an effect on the practice of politics within the state. The nature of the effect of each of the three branches of government on each other has been well studied at the federal level, but much needs to be done at the state level. The major work on the state judiciary in the larger picture of state politics has concerned the efforts of the bar in attempting to implement court reform through changes in the method of judicial recruitment (see, for example, Richard A. Watson and Rondal G. Downing, 1969). However, even the study of the course of judicial review in state supreme courts remains neglected.

Ever since Schmidhauser painted his famous "collective portrait" of the United States Supreme Court, political scientists and students of public law have been interested in the social backgrounds of judges for two reasons. The most basic reason for studying social backgrounds is concern for representation. Although American courts are intended to be insulated from popular pressure, most citizens would not be comfortable with the idea of justice being administered by an elite which does not reflect the diversity of the nation's population. Implicit in this concern for representation is the idea that individuals from different strata in society think and act differently. This is the source of the second reason for interest in judicial biographies. It has been argued that different social backgrounds furnish different kinds of socialization experiences which can help shape a person's attitudes. Attitudes, in turn, become important variables in decision-making for judges as well as other actors. Therefore, if a causal chain can be established between backgrounds and attitudes and attitudes and decision-making on the bench, it will become possible to predict the outcome of cases on the basis of the social backgrounds of the judges. The strength, or even the existence, of this causal chain has been the source of much debate in studies concerning judicial backgrounds.

In 1959, Schmidhauser became the first person to study systematically the lives of United States Supreme Court justices. His primary concern was the representativeness of the justices—the extent to which the members of the Court reflected the diversity of the American population. His findings were not surprising: the Court's membership had an upper class bias as determined by paternal occupation. On the whole, the justices have been white, high-status Protestants of northwestern European ethnic origin. They have been educationally advantaged and from a tradition of politically active families. Schmidhauser suggested that the elite background of the justices may be related to an elite bias in decisions, although he cautioned his readers not to attribute causality to the judicial backgrounds, since such an attribution would ignore subtleties and complexities in decision-making. A few years later, Sheldon Goldman (1965) extended the study of judicial backgrounds to the lower federal courts in a contemporary setting. He found that the lower federal judiciary exhibited more of a middle class, rather than upper class, bias in membership.

The early 1960s brought the first efforts to assess quantitatively the effects of social backgrounds on attitudes and decisions. Stuart Nagel (1962) found some evidence to suggest that political party, religion and ethnic origin were related to liberal and conservative attitudes and decisions. Kenneth N. Vines (1964), in a study of the voting behavior of southern federal judges in desegregation cases, discovered that party, religion, localism and the holding of a state political office were related to decisions. More recently, Sidney S. Ulmer (1970) has found that certain background variables, particularly Catholicism, birthplace and pre-Court career, are related to Supreme Court justices' tendencies to dissent. Goldman (1975) reassessed social backgrounds and voting on the United States Court of Appeals and discovered that political party, age and religion were associated with liberal or conservative decisions in a number of different issue areas. However, these studies, like others concerning the interrelationships among judicial backgrounds, attitudes and decisions, have not been without criticism, and, generally, the actual correlations have been small or even statistically insignificant. While the theory that social backgrounds provide certain socialization experiences which condition attitudes, and that these attitudes are ultimately related to judicial decisions, makes good intuitive sense, the quantitative research is, at best, inconclusive and, at worst, discouraging.

There exists a small but noteworthy subset of the literature concerning judicial backgrounds and voting behavior on state courts of last resort. State supreme courts are of particular interest because of variations among the states in the formal recruitment process of judges. These variations create interesting new problems in the effort to explain voting behavior because of the question of whether or not different recruitment plans succeed in bringing individuals of different social backgrounds to the bench. The relationship between formal judicial recruitment and judicial backgrounds is illustrated by Path E.

In 1971, Dean Jaros and Bradley C. Canon found that judges' characteristics were related to dissent rates on the state supreme courts. A year later, Canon (1972) studied the impact of formal recruitment on the characteristics of 479 state supreme court justices from 1961 to 1968. He identified five basic recruitment plans in use in the states—gubernatorial appointment, legislative election, nonpartisan election, partisan election and "Missouri Plan"—and related them to social background characteristics. Although the analysis was confounded by the interrelationship between region and selection process, Canon uncovered some independent effects of recruitment on some background characteristics, notably religion. In an interview study of the justices of four state supreme courts (Delaware, Maryland, New York and Virginia) chosen, in part, because of the differences in formal recruitment, John T. Wold (1974) found that social backgrounds were related to the role perceptions of the justices. However, Atkins and Glick (1974) found no statistically significant relationships between formal recruitment and decisions in state supreme courts in 1966. They attributed this finding partially to the problem of interim appointment, which can undermine the formal recruitment process, and the notoriously low salience of judicial elections.[10] Consequently, they suggested that researchers stop studying formal recruitments.

Just as in the background studies of the federal judiciary, the studies of judicial backgrounds and decisions of the state supreme courts, even with the added twist of variation in formal recruitment, have produced disappointing results. The relationship between social backgrounds and decisions remains unclear, if, indeed, it does exist at all. Moreover, the justices of the state supreme courts have strikingly similar social backgrounds and career patterns regardless of formal recruitment (Walter A. Borowiec, 1976; Canon, 1971). There is, however, another way of examining judicial backgrounds and understanding the similarities of the judges on state supreme courts.

Polsby has argued:

For a political system to be viable, for it to succeed in performing tasks of authoritative resource allocation, problem solving, conflict settlement, and so on, behalf of a population of any substantial size, it must be institutionalized. That is to say, organizations must be created and sustained that are specialized to political activity. Otherwise, the political system is likely to be unstable, weak and incapable of servicing the demands or protecting the interests of its constituent groups. (1968: 146)

Polsby has developed certain measures to determine the extent to which an organization has become institutionalized. The first measure primarily concerns the channeling of career opportunities so as to create a "well-bounded" system. For Polsby, a well-bounded organization is differentiated from its environment such that:

1. its members are readily identifiable
2. it is relatively difficult to become a member
3. members are recruited principally from within the organization

In an institutionalized organization, Polsby expects that entry will be difficult and turnover infrequent; leadership will professionalize, persist and be recruited from within the organization; and the period of apprenticeship will lengthen.

If state supreme courts are viewed as the leadership of a larger, hierarchically arranged political organziation (i.e., the state judiciary), then the concept of institutionalization becomes useful in explaining the similarities in social backgrounds and career patterns of state supreme court justices, regardless of formal recruitment processes. The different formal recruitment processes should not be viewed as "failures" because they do not succeed in bringing different sorts of legal talent to the bench. Instead, in an institutionalized state judiciary, the very opposite should be true. Formal recruitment plans, whatever they may be, should succeed in securing professional career jurists for the state courts, and this is exactly what they do. (Chapter 3 is devoted, in part, to support of this argument.)

Path E has arrows drawn in both directions because the justices themselves can influence the institutional characteristics of the court system. Schmidhauser (1979) has documented how federal judges and justices have lobbied for the apppointment of particular candidates to the federal bench and changes in the size and staffing of the federal courts. There is at least one well-known case of a state justice working to reform a state judicial system. Justice Arthur Vanderbilt was responsible for constitutional court reform in New Jersey, and Porter (1978) and Glick and Vines (1969) believe that the activist, political nature of the New Jersey Supreme Court can be traced to his efforts.

The study of the role perceptions of state court justices is similar to the study of social background characteristics in that both areas of study are concerned with attitudes that may have an impact on judicial decisions. In 1969, Glick and Vines identified three different role orientations of the state supreme court justices in four states. These orientations—law interpreter, law-maker and "pragmatist"—seemed to be related to the nature of the state political system with the greatest proportion of law-makers found in New Jersey and the smallest in Louisiana. Vines (1969) also distinguished another aspect of the judicial role. He believed that four different conceptions of the primary purpose of the judicial role could be identified. A "ritualist" is a judge who seems preoccupied with the technicalities of litigation; an "adjudicator" believes the primary function of a judge is the resolution of disputes; an "administrator" is a justice who sees the mission of the supreme court as providing guidance for the trial courts; while a "policymaker" is a justice who recognizes and relishes the role of judge-as-legislator for the good of the people. Edward N. Beiser (1974) found the Rhode Island Supreme Court staffed with "administrators" who were committed to the ideals of *stare decisis* and deference to the legislature. Theoretically, role perception should influence decision-making behavior on the bench (Path G), but there has been limited effort to measure the relationship between what justices say they are and what they actually do in decisions. However, in most instances, the researchers are not to be faulted because of the problem of the guarantee of anonymity to the justices.

Beiser has suggested that the role perceptions of state supreme court justices may be important in determining the relationship between the state supreme court and the United States Supreme Court (Path F). Beiser found high consensus on the Rhode Island court on goals, tasks and methods. He found that the justices believed that a state supreme court is an inferior tribunal to the United States Supreme Court in constitutional matters, and, therefore, strict compliance with the federal court's decisions are in order. This finding may be extremely important in helping to explain different levels of state court activism. Obviously, a court staffed with justices with role orientations similar to their colleagues in Rhode Island can scarcely be expected to invoke independent and adequate state constitutional grounds to avoid the requirements of federal law as developed by the United States Supreme Court. Finally, Neil T. Romans (1974) has found a dynamic relationship between state supreme courts and the federal Court. He studied the reaction of state courts of last resort to the decisions in *Escobedo v. Illinois*, 378 U.S. 478, 12 L.Ed.2d 977, 84 S.Ct. 1758 (1964) and *Miranda v. Arizona*, 384 U.S. 436, 16 L.Ed.2d 694, 86 S.Ct. 1602 (1966). Based on his analysis of state court reactions to these two landmark decisions in the field of criminal justice, Romans concluded "the [Supreme] Court is apt to face greater resistance—beyond mere policy preference antagonism—in state courts which have been innovative and less resistance from courts which have been inactive in the areas in which the Court is moving" (1974: 58–59). This finding squares with the work of Beiser. The justices of courts such as Rhode Island perceive their role to be that of an inferior tribunal, and, consequently, ready compliance should be expected from these courts. More importantly, these justices also will be inclined to wait for federal guidance rather than engage in constitutional innovation on their own. Justices on activist state courts very probably have a different perception of the relationship between federal and state courts, and, therefore, resistance and evasion is to be expected from these justices.

Although it may be impossible to alter the role perceptions of sitting justices, it is possible to replace gradually justices in most state supreme courts since the term of office on most courts is only six or eight years. Candidates for a judicial position could be evaluated in terms of their commitment to the development of an independent body of state law, as well as traditional qualifications such as training, experience and character. In this respect, any appointed selection system holds more promise to secure activist state justices than any form of elected system given the minimal amount of information the average voter possesses about candidates for state judicial office.[11]

I have tried to integrate the discrete findings of a number of researchers into a model of some factors related to state supreme court performance in the hope of laying the groundwork for the systematic study of these courts. There exists a kind of conventional wisdom which holds some state supreme courts—notably New Jersey, New York and California—in high esteem as activist courts while regarding other courts as undistinguished. Yet, I am unaware of any quantitative measure capable of ranking the state supreme courts with respect to judicial activism. More importantly, no one has attempted to identify which institutional features of state court systems seem to be most highly associated with judicial activism. This is a most unfortunate situation for both court reformers interested in creating an institutional setting conducive to judicial activism and citizens and attorneys seeking a sympathetic forum for civil liberties litigation. This book represents an initial attempt to understand the sources of variation in state court performance. My work here is far from comprehensive or final. No doubt the proposed model can be subject to modification and the measure of performance improved. However, I believe that this work is a useful contribution to our understanding of what makes courts, or any other political institution, work.

Chapter 2 focuses on variations in the institutional characteristics of state courts. Here I argue that a number of well-known regional variations in the court systems, particularly methods of formal recruitment, are understandable in light of political culture. Chapter 2 also contains a classification scheme for state supreme courts which groups the fifty state supreme courts into six classes according to institutional similarity. Chapter 3 is devoted to an examination of the social and political backgrounds of state supreme court justices in light of the concept of the institutionalization of the state judiciary. Chapter 4 is a study of the dockets of six courts drawn from the classes developed in Chapter 1 in an effort to discover some sources of variation in the performance of the courts. I suggest that differences in state supreme court performance (measured by a judicial activism score, rates of reversals of lower court decisions and levels of disagreement among the justices) may be, in part, attributed to cultural, institutional and personal characteristics. State internal unity and political culture contribute to dissent and reversal rates. Generally, the lower the internal unity, the higher the levels of dissent and reversals will be. The presence of an intermediate appellate court also will contribute to dissents and reversals because the intermediate appellate screening will allow the supreme court to select problematic and important cases for review. The difficult nature of these cases will encourage intracourt disagreement, while the tendency of the supreme court to select cases in which there has been a misapplication of the law will increase the number of reversals of lower court decisions. The characteristics of the justices will contribute further to dissent rates. I propose that a substantial fraction of all dissenting and concurring opinions may be explained in terms of judicial personalities. Certain justices, for unknowable, personal reasons, seem to feel the necessity to write supplementary opinions which seem to add little to the clarification of the court's decisions or the illumination of weaknesses in the majority's legal reasoning. This random factor on certain state supreme courts—the "maverick justice"—may do more to explain dissents and concurrence than institutional or cultural characteristics of the court.

Chapter 5 is devoted to a qualitative assessment of the work of the six state supreme courts. I explain decision-making proclivities in light of the model suggested in this chapter. The chapter attempts to take the reader beyond the simple percentage comparisons of the courts presented in Chapter 4 to an examination of some opinions to illustrate some successes and failures of the model for each of the courts. The concluding chapter summarizes my findings, makes some recommendations for court reform and speculates on the future of state court activism.

A note of caution is in order before proceeding. This book contains the assumption that state court activism—the development of an independent and adequate body of state constitutional law—will be used to enhance the protection of civil rights and liberties of American citizens. The Supremacy Clause of the Federal Constitution prohibits the states from detracting from the minimal standards for the protection of liberties contained in the Bill of Rights as interpreted by the United States Supreme Court. Therefore, it is reasonable to assume that the use of state constitutional grounds implies the creation of a stricter standard for the protection of civil rights and liberties. However, the possibility always remains that state courts will use independent and adequate state grounds to shield decisions from federal review. While the operation of the Supremacy Clause should prevent serious local erosion of civil rights and liberties, the creation of an independent body of state law may promote a provincialism which is anachronistic in an era of instantaneous telecommunications and space travel.

NOTES

1. For a summary of the various approaches to the study of public law see: Sheldon, Charles H. 1974. *The American Judicial Process: Models and Approaches*. New York: Dodd, Mead and Company.

2. Examples of empirical studies of the outcomes and effects of United States Supreme Court decisions may be found in the following collection: Becker, Theodore L., and Malcolm M. Feeley, eds. 1973. *The Impact of Supreme Court Decisions*. New York: Oxford University Press.

3. See, for example: Horowitz, Donald L. 1977. *The Courts and Social Policy*. Washington, D.C.: The Brookings Institution.

4. The *Darby* decision concerned a Georgia lumber manufacturer's challenge to provisions of the Fair Labor Standards Act of 1938. Darby contended that the regulation by Congress of a local activity such as the manufacture of lumber was an unconstitutional extension of the Commerce Power into areas preserved for state regulation by the Tenth Amendment. The Supreme Court, speaking through Justice Stone, rejected Darby's arguments and upheld the act.

The "nationalization" of the Bill of Rights refers to the gradual application of provisions of the first eight amendments of the Constitution to the states as a requirement of the "due process of law" guaranteed by the Fourteenth Amendment. The Bill of Rights was originally understood to apply only to the federal government. See: *Barron v. Mayor and City Council of Baltimore*, 32 U.S. (7 Pet.) 243, 8 L.Ed. 672 (1833).

5. The *National League of Cities* case involved a challenge to 1974 amendments to the Fair Labor Standards Act which extended coverage of the act to certain classes of state and municipal employees. A plurality of the Supreme Court, speaking through Justice Rehnquist, held that a newly revitalized Tenth Amendment prohibited congressional regulations of states in their capacities as units of government. However, *National League of Cities* has since been overruled in a five-four decision of the Court in *Garcia v. San Antonio Metropolitan Transit Authority*, 469 U.S. 528, 105 S.Ct. 1005, 83 L.Ed.2d 1016 (1985). Justice Rehnquist remains confident that his views announced in *National League of Cities* "will . . . in time again command the support of a majority of this Court."

6. A six-member majority of the Supreme Court held in *Stone v. Powell* that:

where the state has provided an opportunity for full and fair litigation of a Fourth Amendment claim, the Constitution does not require that a state prisoner be granted federal habeas corpus relief on the ground that evidence obtained in an unconstitutional search or seizure was introduced at his trial. (428 U.S. 465, 482)

Justice Powell's views on the issue of parity between federal and state courts are summarized in footnote 35 of his opinion for the court:

Despite differences in institutional environment and the unsympathetic attitude to federal constitutional claims of some state judges in past years, we are unwilling to assume that there now exists a general lack of appropriate sensitivity to constitutional rights . . . in courts of the several States . . . There is no intrinsic reason why the fact a man is a federal judge should make him more competent, or conscientious, or learned . . . than his neighbor in the state court house. (428 U.S. 465, 494 fn. 35)

7. The other two factors are "sectionalism" and the concept of the "frontier." The following discussion of political culture is drawn entirely from Elazar's work.

8. For a description of the different administrative styles in the states see: Tobin, Robert W., and Richard B. Hoffman. 1979. *The Administrative Role of Chief Justices and Supreme Courts*. National Center for State Courts: Publication No. 10046.

9. For a critical review of some of the research available in organizational theory see: Perrow, Charles. 1979. *Complex Organizations: A Critical Essay*, 2d ed. Glenview, Ill.: Scott, Foresman and Company.

10. The extent of the problem of interim appointment is revealed in Herndon, James. 1962. Appointment as a Means of Initial Accession to Elective State Courts of Last Resort. *North Dakota Law Review*, 38:60–73.

11. For analyses of voting in judicial election see: Adamany, David W., and Philip DuBois. 1976. Electing State Judges. *Wisconsin Law Review*, 3:371–78; Barber, Kathleen. 1971. Ohio Elections—Nonpartisan Premises with Partisan Results. *Ohio State Law Journal*, 32:762–89; DuBois, Philip L. 1980. *From Ballot to Bench: Judicial Elections and the Quest for Accountability*. Austin: University of Texas Press; DuBois, Philip L. 1979. The Significance of Voting Cues in State Supreme Court Elections. *Law and Society Review*, 13:757–78; DuBois, Philip L. 1979. Voter Turnout in State Judicial Elections: An Analysis of the Tail on the Electoral Kite. *Journal of Politics*, 41:865–87; Landinsky, Jack, and Allan Silver. 1967. Popular Democracy and Judicial Independence: Electorate and Elite Reactions to Two Wisconsin Supreme Court Elections. *Wisconsin Law Review*, 1967:128–69.

2. Institutional Characteristics of State Supreme Courts

In Chapter 1, I developed a model of some factors related to state supreme court performance. This model, in essence, contains the hypothesis that variations in state supreme court performance can be explained by two kinds of variables: institutional and contextual. I have suggested that the institutional characteristics of the state court system, such as the presence or absence of an intermediate appellate court, will have some effect on the kinds of decisions rendered by a state court of last resort. Furthermore, the determination of the effect of institutional characteristics on decision-making should be the focus of study by social scientists and court reformers simply because these structures can be modified in the interest of improving court performance. However, organizations do not exist in a vacuum—they are, in part, products of and dependent upon their environment.[1] Here is where non-institutional (or "contextual") variables come into play. Socioeconomic development and political culture will condition and limit the practice of politics in the state and will help to shape the structure of political organizations. In this chapter, I examine variations in the institutional characteristics of state court systems. The first section of the chapter is almost purely descriptive of differences among the fifty court systems. Here I also hope to demonstrate the need for a classification scheme for state court systems to simplify the study of these courts. I then study regional variations in institutional characteristics to illustrate the relationship between political culture and institutions as suggested in my model. Finally, I develop a sixfold classification scheme based upon institutional similarity for state supreme courts.

THE DATA BASE AND SOME METHODOLOGICAL NOTES

The data for this chapter and subsequent chapters describing the institutional characteristics of the fifty state judicial systems were drawn from the 1976 and 1978 editions of *State Court Systems*, a publication of the Council of State Governments.[2] A total of forty-five variables were coded for both years. These variables included:

1. the organization of the state courts
2. the number of justices and judges serving in the state courts
3. the formal qualifications for judicial office
4. methods of removal of judges and justices
5. salaries for supreme court justices and the chief justice
6. methods of formal recruitment for judges and justices
7. legal and clerical assistance furnished the court of last resort
8. conference procedures used by the court of last resort (including the order of discussion, voting and opinion assignment)[3]

Throughout the remainder of this book, I use geographic region as defined by the United States Census Bureau as a crude indicator of political culture. Elazar (1966) has noted how the three major political cultures form imperfect geographical patterns. Generally, the Individualistic culture prevails in the northeastern states, the Traditionalistic dominates in the South and the Moralistic in the Midwest. The western states' culture is problematic even for Elazar. However, it is safe to say that most of the states west of the Rocky Mountains embody varying mixtures of the Individualistic and Moralistic cultures. Arizona and New Mexico are exceptions since they may be classified as Traditionalistic and Moralistic.[4] I have chosen to use census region as an indicator of political culture partly because few states exhibit pure cultural types and partly because it is necessary to keep the number of classifications for states small in order to avoid the problems of small marginals and empty cells in crosstabulations. There are also some difficulties with the validity of Elazar's classification of political cultures. His identification of cultures is almost completely determined by impressionistic evidence. While Elazar (1970) does use some census data (such as population density, employment and family and household information) in mapping his civic communities, the bulk of his data is derived from a subjective examination of public documents, newspapers and interviews with selected citizens and government officials.[5] Given the problem of validity in Elazar's classification of political cultures and the practical need for small numbers of categories, I believe census region is a sound choice for a surrogate indicator of political culture.

VARIATIONS IN STATE COURT ORGANIZATION

Excluding the federal judiciary, there are as many court systems in this country as there are states in the Union. The differences among the states extend to every aspect of state court organizations. The structure, number and degree of specialization of courts, the number of judges and justices and the formal procedures used to govern the selection and supervision of the judiciary are but a few examples of the scope of variation in state court systems. There are variations in the hierarchical relations of courts to each other within a state, and there are variations across states in the structure and procedures associated with courts similarly situated in the judicial hierarchy.

An examination of state supreme courts can provide numerous examples of the variations among the states in a single kind of court.[6] The number of justices on a state's supreme court varies from a low of three to a high of nine with five and seven justices as the modal categories. The term of office for a justice ranges from six years to life appointment in the single case of Rhode Island, the only state which provides the ultimate in job security. The terms of office for state supreme court justices are summarized on Table 2.1.

Judicial salaries are another source of difference among state courts

Table 2.1 Term of Office, Courts of Last Resort, 1976, 1978

Term (years)	1976	1978
6-8	56.0%	56.0%
10-15	36.0	36.0
age 70-life	8.0	8.0

of last resort. In 1976, the justices of the Mississippi Supreme Court arguably were underpaid at $26,000 per year, while the justice of the California Supreme Court earned a salary of more than $62,000 per year, a figure which included a built-in, annual cost-of-living increase. The average salary for all justices in 1976 was $37,918. By 1978, the mean had increased to $41,947. Unlike the federal model, only twenty-eight states in 1976 and thirty states in 1978 offered a supplementary salary to the chief justice.

State supreme courts also differ in formal recruitment processes. In 1976 and 1978, there were ten different formal recruitment mechanisms in operation in the states. The most popular formal recruitment processes were partisan and nonpartisan election of judges, although the Missouri Plan is slowly becoming the dominant method of judicial selection. The plan features initial gubernatorial appointment from "merit" lists of candidates chosen by a judicial nominating commission. The newly appointed justice subsequently stands for retention at an election on his or her record after a short, specified period of time. For the past forty years, any major change in formal recruitment in the states has been shifted to some form of merit selection to replace partisan or nonpartisan election. In 1976, there was a single legislative appointment state (Connecticut), three states whose plans required gubernatorial appointment with legislative consent along the lines of the federal model (Delaware, Hawaii and New Jersey) and three states with legislative election of justices (Rhode Island, South Carolina and Virginia). Three states used what could be considered a variation on the federal model: Maine, Massachusetts and New Hampshire required the governor's appointment to be ratified by the executive council. California maintained a unique method of formal recruitment—gubernatorial appointment with approval by a judicial council, followed by a retention election on the justice's record. The variations in formal recruitment in the states are summarized in Table 2.2.

A comparison of institutional characteristics reveals additional differences in state court systems. Only 52 percent of the states maintained intermediate appellate courts in 1978. While 80 percent of the states in 1978 had a single trial court of general jurisdiction, more than half included more than the three courts of limited jurisdiction. Texas and Arkansas arguably shared the dubious distinction of maintaining the most byzantine court systems in the nation. The 1978 Arkansas system included six courts of limited jurisdiction, two trial

Table 2.2 Formal Judicial Recruitment in the States, 1976, 1978

	1976	1978
"Missouri Plan"	18.0%	20.0%
"California Plan"	2.0	2.0
Legislative Appointment	2.0	2.0
Gubernatorial Appointment with Legislative Consent	6.0	8.0
Non-partisan Election	28.0	24.0
Partisan Election	24.0	22.0
Gubernatorial Appointment with Retention Election[1]	2.0	2.0
Legislative Election	6.0	6.0
Gubernatorial Appointment from "Merit" List[2]	6.0	6.0
Gubernatorial Appointment with Executive Council Consent	6.0	4.0

[1] No "merit list"

[2] No retention election

courts of general jurisdiction, no intermediate appellate court and a court of last resort. In the same year, Texas maintained ten limited jurisdiction courts, a single trial court and a completely bifurcated system of appeals. Criminal cases are tried in district court and appealed in the Supreme Court of Criminal Appeals, while civil cases also begin in district court but are appealed to an intermediate Court of Civil Appeals and, ultimately, to the Supreme Court. If organizational charts were made for the judicial systems of the fifty states, it would become apparent that there is no such thing as a "typical" state court system.

The states also differ in their efforts to remove politics and corruption from the administration of justice. Merit systems of judicial selection (i.e., systems which restrict initial appointment of justices to a list of qualified candidates drawn up by a judicial nominating commission) are becoming common at the appellate court level. However, merit systems have only begun to penetrate the lower levels of courts. By 1978, 60 percent of all selection systems for state supreme court justices contained a merit element, but only 22 percent of formal recruitment plans for trial judges had a merit element. Merit selection of judges is completely absent at the level of courts of limited jurisdiction where minimal qualifications for judicial office are the rule and non-lawyer magistrates remain common. An increasingly common feature of state court systems is the use of judicial qualifications commissions to supervise the conduct of judges and justices. However, just as in the case of merit selection, the use of these commissions is most common at the appellate level, while the court of last resort retains primary supervisory authority of trial court judges. The variations in selected institutional characteristics of state court systems are summarized in Table 2.3.

The state judicial systems are also different in the number of judges and justices serving on the state courts. Of course, the number of judicial offices in a state is a function of the state's population. The

Table 2.3 Variations in Institutional Characteristics, 1976, 1978

States with:	1976	1978
Intermediate Appellate Court	40.0%	52.0%
Single General Jurisdiction Trial Court	82.0	80.0
0-2 Limited Jurisdiction Courts	42.0	44.0
Merit Element in Court of Last Resort Recruitment	28.0	34.0
Merit Element in Trial Court Judge Recruitment	18.0	22.0
Supplementary Salary for Chief Justice	56.0	60.0
Judicial Qualifications Commission Trial Judge Supervision	28.0	32.0
Judicial Qualifications Commission Court of Last Resort Supervision	56.0	66.0

most populous states, California and New York, have the greatest number of judges, while the states with the smallest number of residents, Wyoming and Alaska, have the least. A more interesting phenomenon is the amount of legal and clerical assistance provided to the state's supreme court. Generally, each state supreme court justice has the assistance of at least one law clerk. However, the seven justices of the California Supreme Court had the benefit of thirty-three law clerks to assist with legal research in 1978. With the unfortunate exception of Utah, all state supreme courts had special secretarial and clerical assistance although there was quite a wide range of staffing patterns. In 1978, Pennsylvania came out on top in secretaries and Texas in additional clerical staff. The five justices of the Utah Supreme Court must be awash in paperwork: they have no secretarial staff of their own but are able to borrow "three girls in the clerk's office."[7] The differences in the number of staff members serving the state supreme courts are summarized in Table 2.4.

REGIONAL VARIATIONS IN STATE COURT SYSTEMS

Chapter 1 presented a number of hypotheses concerning the relationship between political culture and institutional characteristics of the state court systems. By way of review, the Individualistic culture is expected to exhibit a large, bureaucratized court system, staffed by highly paid, career judges selected on a partisan basis. The Moralistic culture, with its intolerance of corruption and emphasis on civic duty, should feature judicial selection by merit systems or nonpartisan election and strict supervision of the courts by judicial commission, as well as low-salaried judges. Finally, the Traditionalistic culture, with its stress on the maintenance of historic patterns and a hierarchical society, should preserve old, unstreamlined systems of courts.

In order to confirm these hypotheses, a series of crosstabulations were run using geographical region as a surrogate for political culture. The results were mixed. There was no statistically significant relationship between judicial salaries and political culture or court structure (i.e., the presence of an intermediate appellate court, the number of limited jurisdiction courts) and political culture. However, in both 1976 and 1978, there was a relationship between formal recruitment and political culture. Tables 2.5 and 2.6 indicate that nonpartisan

Table 2.4 Staffing the State Courts, 1976, 1978

Variable	1976			1978		
	Range	Mean	Median	Range	Mean	Median
Justices, Intermediate Appellate Courts	0-56	8.96	0.46	0-56	10.0	5.17
Judges, General Jurisdiction Trial Courts	7-610	109.60	67.50	13-650	121.26	75.5
Law Clerks, Courts of Last Resort	3-32	9.32	8.25	3-33	10.38	9.0
Secretaries, Courts of Last Resort	0-14	7.00	7.90	2-25	7.50	7.0
Supplementary Staff, Courts of Last Resort	0-16	2.3	0.5	0-30	6.32	4.5

Table 2.5 Regional Variations in Formal Judicial Recruitment, 1976

	Appointment	Mixed[1]	Nonpartisan Election	Partisan Election
North	70.0%	0.0%	0.0%	30.0%
South	0.0	13.3	20.0	66.7
Midwest	8.3	33.3	50.0	8.3
West	15.4	38.5	38.5	7.7

significance = 0.000[2]

lambda = 0.37

Table 2.6 Regional Variations in Formal Judicial Recruitment, 1978

	Appointment	Mixed[1]	Nonpartisan Election	Partisan Election
North	70.0%	10.0%	0.0%	20.0%
South	0.0	20.0	20.0	60.0
Midwest	8.3	33.3	50.0	8.3
West	15.4	46.2	30.8	7.7

significance = 0.000[2]

lambda = 0.39

[1] "Mixed" recruitment plans feature initial gubernatorial appointment with or without the benefit of a merit list, and a subsequent retention election.

[2] Statistical significance has been determined by Chi-square test. The significance level should be interpreted with caution because all the cells in this table have expected cell frequencies of less than 5.0.

election and "mixed" systems of judicial selection predominated in the Midwest and West. Here, "mixed" systems are recruitment plans which require initial gubernatorial appointment, with or without the benefit of merit lists, and a subsequent retention election on the justice's record. The partisan election of judges was primarily a southern phenomenon, although one southern state, Florida, changed to the Missouri Plan in 1978. Finally, appointment of judges is, for the large part, localized on the northern region of the nation. The correlation between region and formal recruitment, measured by lambda (which is appropriate to nominal levels of measurement) was 0.37 in 1976 and 0.39 in 1978.

The regional patterns in formal judicial recruitment reflect the historical and political development of the states. These historical and political factors contribute to political culture. Some older, northeastern states maintain plans by which the governor appoints all state judges. These states remained within the old colonial tradition of a strong, crown-appointed executive. Other East Coast states use legislative election to choose judges. This approach reflects a concern, also rooted in the colonial experience, over concentration of power in the executive. Election of judges is found in southern and midwestern states where Jacksonian Democracy and later the Populist Movement were strong. Originally, almost every one of the elective states used partisan election of judges. However, as political parties increasingly became associated with the corrupt politics of the smoke-filled room, a number of states, particularly those of the Moralistic Midwest, moved to the nonpartisan election of judges. The Missouri Plan is found in midwestern and western states where a strong bar association was interested in improving the quality of administration of justice by way of reform of judicial recruitment. This reform movement, like the movement of nonpartisan election judges, is consistent with moralistic values.[8]

In Chapter 1, I hypothesized that a merit element in judicial selection and the use of judicial qualifications commissions for the supervision of the judiciary would be associated with the moralistic political culture. To confirm these hypotheses, I crosstabulated region with merit selection and the use of judicial qualifications commissions. Although the results are not statistically significant, they are suggestive. A merit element in the selection of both trial and appellate justices was most often found in the Midwest and West. The use of judicial qualifica-

Institutional Characteristics 35

tions commissions was also found most often in midwestern and western states. By 1978, 92.3 percent of all western states had judicial qualifications commissions to supervise trial court judges. In only one instance did a non-moralistic culture use qualifications commissions more frequently than Moralistic cultures. By 1978, the use of qualifications commissions to supervise the state's court of last resort had become more common in the Traditionalistic South than anywhere else. The results of the crosstabulation are presented in Table 2.7.

A CLASSIFICATION SYSTEM FOR STATE SUPREME COURTS

Given the variety of state courts, the development of a classification scheme for state court systems would be a useful preliminary step in their study. The new judicial federalism requires state supreme courts to take on increased responsibility in constitutional interpretation in general and the development of a tradition of state constitutional interpretation in particular. However, as discussed in Chapter 1, some scholars, notably Neuborne (1977), believe that state courts suffer from certain institutional deficiencies which prevent them from serving as the functional equivalents to federal courts. Such a belief is a gross oversimplification due to the inherent assumption that all state court systems are alike. They very clearly are not. Here, I would like to suggest a classification scheme for state courts to group states according to similarities in institutional characteristics as a first step toward evaluating the capacity of state courts to serve as functional equivalents to the federal courts.

Other researchers have engaged in the comparative study of state supreme courts and have attempted to develop typologies for them. One of the few comprehensive studies of state courts was done by Kagan et al. (1978). These investigators were interested in determining how increasing caseload affected the structure and business of state court systems from 1870 to 1970. A sample of sixteen states was chosen on the basis of certain demographic and geographical variables to represent the United States. Then, a random sample was drawn from all the opinions issued by the supreme courts of the sixteen states, and these opinions were divided into four crude categories: property cases (including contracts, collection and corporate law), criminal and public law cases, private torts (excluding workmen's compensation) and

Table 2.7 Regional Variations in Judicial Selection and Supervision, 1976, 1978

1976[1]

Variable	North	South	Midwest	West
Merit Element: Court of Last Resort[2]	20.0%	6.7%	41.7%	46.2%
Merit Element: Trial Courts	20.0	0.0	25.0	30.8
Trial Judge Removal via Judicial Commission	30.0	13.3	25.0	38.5
Trial Judge Supervision via Judicial Commission	50.0	60.0	91.7	85.6
Court of Last Resort Supervision via Judicial Commission	40.0	60.0	66.7	53.8

1978[1]

Variable	North	South	Midwest	West
Merit Element: Court of Last Resort[2]	30.0%	13.3%	41.7%	53.8%
Merit Element: Trial Courts	20.0	6.7	25.0	38.5
Trial Judge Removal via Judicial Commission	20.0	33.3	25.0	46.2
Trial Judge Supervision via Judicial Commission	50.0	73.3	83.3	92.3
Court of Last Resort Supervision via Judicial Commission	50.0	73.3	66.7	69.2

[1] In no instance are the results statistically significant at the 0.5 level.

[2] A selection system has a "merit element" if the governor's choice in filling the office is restricted to the nominees appearing on a limited list of candidates approved by a judicial nominating commission.

constitutional cases. Kagan et al. noticed how the nature of the issues addressed by the state courts changed as the state developed politically and economically. Futhermore, they found that the usual response to increased caseload was the creation of an intermediate court of appeals. This change, in turn, was related to increased discretion in case selection by the supreme court and a change in the nature of the issues addressed by the court. In general, supreme courts with the benefit of an intermediate appellate screening of cases usually dealt with more pressing issues, such as constitutional claims, in their decisions. On the basis of these findings, the reseachers formulated a fourfold typology of state supreme courts using the state's population and the degree of discretion allowed its supreme court in choosing cases for review.

The Kagan et al. study provides a good foundation for future research. The results indicate that institutional changes in a court system should be expected when caseload increases and that these changes should be related to changes in the nature of the business of the supreme court. This finding also suggests it would be profitable to examine additional institutional features in a court system to see whether supreme courts assisted by a modern lower court structure, for example, are more likely to deal with constitutional cases. It would also be useful to refine the case classification system used by Kagan et al. to determine whether or not state courts are becoming increasingly active in the areas suggested by Justice Brennan: equal protection, due process and criminal justice.

Atkins and Glick (1976) have compared state supreme courts using an Eastonian systems model. These researchers believe that "since courts are passive rather than active policymakers, the characteristics of the socioeconomic and political environment which generate demands and conflicts may be important predictors of the kinds of issues resolved by judicial institutions." To test this hypothesis, Atkins and Glick classified state supreme court cases as: criminal justice, civil liberties, economic regulation, private economic litigation and private non-economic litigation. These dependent variables were correlated with variables describing a state's political and economic environment. The results were disappointing. Atkins and Glick found some relationship between the environmental variables and the cases, but they believed the relationship to have been obscured by multicollinearity among the environmental variables. Generally, supreme courts in rural states tended to have a greater proportion of private litigation, while states scoring high on affluence and economic development tended to have supreme courts which were more involved in economic regulation and civil liberties litigation.

Atkins and Glick included one court system variable in their study—the presence or absence of an intermediate appellate court. They discovered that intermediate appellate courts were more likely to be found in politically and economically developed states, and the presence of intermediate appellate courts was related to an increase in the proportion of criminal cases appearing in supreme court. This finding, once again, suggests that additional court systems variables be included in a study of the work of state supreme courts. Finally, Atkins and Glick believe that a refined system of case classification is needed, and they argue for such a system in order to separate constitutional from nonconstitutional issues, especially in criminal appeals.

Vines and Jacob (1971) also have used an Eastonian systems model to study state courts. However, unlike Atkins and Glick, these researchers have focused almost exclusively on variables which describe court structure. Vines and Jacob developed a number of means by which courts systems may be classified. One method divides court systems according to the structure of the lower courts. Court systems approximating the American Bar Association's model (single trial court of general jurisdiction, intermediate appellate court, court of last resort with the power of discretionary review) are "simple and modern," while court systems featuring numerous limited jurisdiction courts, multiple trial courts and no intermediate appellate court are "complex and traditional." Vines and Jacob place two hybrid systems between the traditional and modern extremes. Another method classified courts by judicial recruitment plan. Courts were placed along a five-point scale ranking the recruitment plans (partisan election, election by legislature, appointment, Missouri Plan, and nonpartisan election) according to the relative degrees of party and bar association influence. Finally, Vines and Jacob rated state court systems according to a legal professionalism score based on a combination of variables describing judicial recruitment, tenure of office and court organization. However, this study, much like the similar effort by Glick and Vines (1973), used the legal professionalism score to assess the impact of the organized bar on court reform rather than evaluate the effect of institutional structure on the ability of courts to render decisions efficiently and carefully.

Neuborne's reservations concerning the adequacy of state supreme courts to process constitutional claims and, indeed, the major premise behind arguments for court reform contain the underlying assumption that certain institutions will be "better" at performing some tasks than other institutions.[9] In the context of this assumption, "better" usually has been used to describe the more efficient functioning of courts in terms of handling a given caseload with minimal delay and expenditures of time and money, although Chief Justice Arthur Englander of the Florida Supreme Court is willing to extend this definition to the creation of "good public policy."[10] The scholarly research cited earlier indicates that at least the presence or absence of an intermediate appellate court is related to changes in the work of the state supreme court. Therefore, it is reasonable to hypothesize that additional structural characteristics may be related to the nature of a supreme court's caseload and decisions. The problem now becomes the selection of the appropriate institutional characteristics by which to classify state courts. It was hoped that state supreme courts could be classified along two dimensions, forming six to eight categories. Fewer categories would be too broad and do little to distinguish among the courts, while more than eight classes would lead to the problem of small marginals and empty cells in any analysis using crosstabulation.

Political scientists have frequently classified state supreme courts according to judicial recruitment plan. (See, for example, Atkins and Glick, 1974; Canon, 1972). This has been done for two reasons. First, variations in judicial recruitment plans follow a well-known regional pattern which reflects the historical and political development of the states. Second, it has been argued that different recruitment plans attract to the bench individuals with different kinds of judicial and political experience. Opponents of gubernatorial appointment and partisan election of judges have suggested that these plans fill the bench with a disproportionate share of "political cronies" and "party hacks." Critics of the Missouri Plan have averred that all this "so-called merit plan" succeeds in doing is strengthening the hold of the bar association on judgeships and creating a judicial aristocracy in the United States. Although quantitative research has been remarkably unsuccessful in distinguishing judicial backgrounds and decision outcomes by judicial recruitment (see, for example, Atkins and Glick, 1974; Wold, 1974; Canon, 1973; Jacob, 1964), the relationship between formal recruitment and state political culture provides a sound reason for including method of formal recruitment as one dimension of a state court classification system.

Once it was determined to use method of formal recruitment as the first dimension along which state supreme courts may be classified, it became necessary to evaluate states according to their individual recruitment plans and group them into categories. Although recruitment plans are usually placed in one of three, four or five categories, there were actually ten different plans in use in 1976 and 1978. Given the variety of selection plans and the determination that judicial recruitment would form only one dimension of the classification system, it became necessary to collapse categories and decide upon some criterion for assigning each plan to a particular category. The criterion chosen was the degree of popular control of the recruitment of judges, with popular control defined as the presence of an election somewhere in the recruitment process. Using this criterion, the ten selection plans were collapsed into three categories: purely appointive plans (by either the governor or the legislature, with or without merit lists), mixed plans (appointment, with or without merit lists, combined with a retention election), and purely elective plans (either partisan, nonpartisan or legislative election).

Seven other variables were now selected as candidates for the other dimension of the court classification system. Four variables concern the structure and size of the state's lower court systems. These variables were chosen for two reasons. First, the bulk of every state supreme court's jurisdiction is appellate; thus, facts will be found and legal issues framed in the lower trial courts. Second, if a supreme court has the benefit of an intermediate appellate court's screening of cases, then the supreme court will be able to select cases for final review which have the greatest potential legal, social, economic or political impact. These considerations suggest that lower court structure may be related to the nature of the supreme court's docket. Next, a state supreme court is the apex of the state judicial system, and the court or the chief justice is vested with administrative authority over the bar and the bench.[11] A court or a chief justice with administrative authority over a large lower court system may be particularly sensitive to the politics of court funding and judicial selection and the necessity to work closely with the legislative and executive branches of state government. The consequences of the politics of court administration may be reflected in a court of justices with previous political experience or in decisions which are especially attuned to the political, economic and social conditions within a state. For these reasons, it is appropriate to include lower court variables in the development of a classification system for state supreme courts. The following lower court variables were used: number of judges on intermediate appellate courts, number of judges on trial courts of general jurisdiction, number of types of trial courts of general jurisdiction and number of limited jurisdiction courts.

The remaining variables included in the development of the classification system are directly related to the supreme court. The first of these variables was the salary of the justices, and the reason for its use is obvious. It has long been argued that high salaries will provide the incentive for talented lawyers to leave private practice for public service. The second variable was the number of technical and clerical personnel provided the court to assist in its work. Although the number of law clerks, secretaries and supplementary staff members was originally coded separately, the three job categories were added together to form a single variable which could be called support staff. This procedure was done to avoid the problem of different job definitions, especially in the secretarial and supplementary staff categories, in comparing the states between the years 1976 and 1978. The support staff variable was included because it is reasonable to assume that courts provided with a large clerical staff will be able to process applications for review and report opinions quickly, thereby decreasing delays and case backlog. The final variable chosen was the term of office of supreme court justices, and the reason for its use is again apparent. The conventional wisdom holds that the longer the term of office, the greater the insulation from majoritarian pressures and the greater the independence of the judiciary.[12]

Since all seven variables were interval level, factor analysis was used to discover whether it was possible to reduce the seven variables to one or more underlying dimensions. This statistical technique is ideal for the creation of a classification system for state supreme courts because it is "based on the fundamental assumption that some underlying factors, which are smaller in number than the observed variables, are responsible for the covariation among the observed variables" (Jae-On

Kim and Charles W. Mueller, 1978a: 12). Thus, variables which are part of the same underlying factor can be combined and the classification system based on the variables, simplified. This particular use of factor analysis is called "exploratory." In exploratory factor analysis, the researcher has no "idea as to how many underlying dimensions there are for the data," so the statistical technique is invoked to "ascertain the minimum number of hypothetical factors that can account for the observed covariation" in the data (Kim and Mueller, 1978b: 9). In 1976, support staff, the number of judges on intermediate appellate courts and trial courts and salaries loaded high on a single factor, while only the number of courts of limited jurisdiction loaded high on another. This finding suggested that the four variables could be reduced to a single dimension which could be called system size. The results for 1978 were similar to 1976. Again, support staff, number of judges on intermediate appellate courts and trial courts and salaries loaded high on a single factor and limited jurisdiction courts on another. Table A.1, which appears in the appendix, presents the results of the factor analysis.

Based on the results of the factor analysis, support staff, the number of judges on intermediate appellate and trial courts and salaries were combined into a single variable—system size—according to the following formula:

> System Size = Support Staff + Judges Intermediate Courts
> + Judges Trial Courts + Salary/100 (rounded to the nearest whole number).

Salaries were divided by 100 to bring them within the same order of magnitude of the other variables in the equation. This new variable, system size, was to become the second dimension of the supreme court classification system.[13] The system scores for 1976 ranged from 286 to 1214 with a median of 467.5, while in 1978, the scores ranged from 318 to 1298 with a median of 521.5. The median for each year was used to divide the state supreme courts into two convenient groups of twenty-five. State supreme courts scoring less than the median on system size were ranked "low," and those scoring above the median were ranked "high." These rankings formed the second dimension of the court classification system.[14] When the system ranking is combined with the method of judicial selection, a sixfold classification

Institutional Characteristics 43

system results. The final classifications of the states for 1976 and 1978 are presented in Tables 2.8 and 2.9.

In this chapter, I hope to have demonstrated the variety of state court systems, the way in which certain institutional features of state courts are related to political culture and the need for a classification scheme for state supreme courts. This chapter contains two original contributions to our understanding of state supreme courts. First, I believe I have added to our knowledge of the relationship between political culture and the institutional characteristics of state courts. Other researchers have noted the relationship between geographical region and formal recruitment process, but no one has discussed this phenomenon explicitly in terms of political culture. Moreover, I have examined additional facets of the state judiciary, notably merit elements in judicial selection and qualifications commissions in judicial supervision, in terms of political culture. Although the relationships between political culture and institutions are imperfect, like all relationships in social science, the concept of culture is useful in explaining regional variations in state court systems. I also believe I have succeeded in treating political culture as a legitimate independent variable. In Chapter 1, I noted how contextual variables frequently are treated as explanations of last resort. When all other sources of variation have been examined and found deficient, an appeal is made to political culture. I have avoided this pitfall by starting with some hypotheses on how cultural types should be related to institutional characteristics and then attempting to confirm them.

Second, I believe I have succeeded in creating a useful, sixfold classification system for state supreme courts based on institutional similarity. The classification system also captures elements of political culture in its use of method of formal recruitment as one of the dimensions along which the states are grouped. For example, all Class I states, with the single exception of Delaware, have a Moralistic element in their political cultures according to Elazar, as do all Class II and Class V states with the exception of Missouri and Oklahoma.[15] Virtually all the states with Traditionalistic aspects to their culture are found in Classes III and VI, while Class IV is made up of purely Individualistic states. Of course, other means by which state courts may be classified can be developed, and this particular method only succeeds in creating relative ranking of the states. However, I believe the ultimate utility of this method lies in its ability to incorporate the institutional and

Table 2.8 The 1976 Court Classes: Method of Selection

System Score Below Median		
Appointment CLASS I	Missouri Plan CLASS II	Election CLASS III
Arizona	Kansas	Arkansas	North Carolina
Connecticut	Nebraska	Idaho	North Dakota
Delaware	Utah	Kentucky	Oregon
Maine	Wyoming	Minnesota	Rhode Island
New Hampshire		Mississippi	South Carolina
Vermont		Montana	South Dakota
		Nevada	West Virginia
		New Mexico	

System Score Above Median		
CLASS IV	CLASS V	CLASS VI
Hawaii	Alaska	Alabama	Ohio
Indiana	California	Florida	Pennsylvania
Massachusetts	Colorado	Georgia	Tennessee
New Jersey	Iowa	Illinois	Texas
	Maryland	Louisiana	Virginia
	Missouri	Michigan	Washington
	Oklahoma	New York	Wisconsin

Table 2.9 The 1978 Court Classes: Method of Selection

System Score Below Median		
Appointment CLASS I	Missouri Plan CLASS II	Election CLASS III
Arizona	Idaho	Alabama	North Dakota
Connecticut	Missouri	Arkansas	Oregon
Delaware	Nebraska	Kentucky	Rhode Island
Hawaii	Utah	Mississippi	South Carolina
Maine	Vermont	Montana	South Dakota
Massachusetts	Wyoming	Nevada	West Virginia
New Hampshire		New Mexico	Wisconsin

System Score Above Median		
CLASS IV	CLASS V	CLASS VI
Indiana	Alaska	Georgia	Ohio
New Jersey	California	Illinois	Pennsylvania
New York	Colorado	Louisiana	Tennessee
	Florida	Michigan	Texas
	Iowa	Minnesota	Virginia
	Kansas	North Carolina	Washington
	Maryland		
	Oklahoma		

cultural elements which are the essence of the model of the factors related to state supreme court performance presented in Chapter 1. The next chapter examines the social and political backgrounds of the justices of the state supreme courts.

NOTES

1. Of course, organizations will also seek to influence their environment, and it would be a mistake to view organizations such as courts as completely passive bodies existing in a cultural environment that controls all their actions. The most notable example of courts seeking to exert some control over their environment can be seen in efforts to regulate caseload. Trial court judges will lobby for increased judgeships, more clerical assistance and better procedures for docketing cases. Court of last resort justices will ask for legislation to increase discretion in the selection of cases as well as additional lower court judges. Descriptions of the way in which organizations seek to control their environment may be found in: Perrow, Charles. 1979. *Complex Organizations: A Critical Essay*, 2d ed. Glenview, Ill.: Scott, Foresman and Company; Scott, Richard W. 1981. *Organizations: Rational, Natural and Open Systems*. Englewood Cliffs, N.J.: Prentice-Hall, Inc.

2. The Council of State Government ceased publication of *State Court Systems* with the 1978 edition. Subsequent editions are available from the National Center for State Courts.

3. This information in conference procedures was drawn from: McConkie, Stanford S. 1976. Decision-Making in the State Supreme Courts. *Judicature*, 59:337–43.

4. The dominant political cultures by states according to Elazar may be found in the 1966 edition of *American Federalism: A View from the States*. New York: Thomas Y. Crowell, p. 108.

5. A description of Elazar's methodology is available in the appendices to his 1970 work: *Cities of the Prairie: The Metropolitan Frontier and American Politics*. New York: Basic Books, Inc.

6. Both Texas and Oklahoma have two co-equal courts of last resort, one for criminal and one for civil appeals. This book only considers the court of civil appeals to avoid duplication.

7. This quotation is from the report on staffing given by the Utah Court to the compilers of the 1976 edition of *State Court Systems*.

8. Good summaries of the histories of different judicial selection plans may be found in: DuBois, Philip L. 1980. *From Ballot to Bench: Judicial Elections and the Quest for Accountability*. Austin: University of Texas Press; Watson, Richard A., and Rondal G. Downing. 1969. *The Politics of the Bench*

and the Bar: Judicial Selection under the Missouri Nonpartisan Court Plan. New York: John Wiley and Sons, Inc.

9. Numerous examples of the use of this assumption can be seen in the report available in: Powell, Lee, ed. 1980. *Court Reform in Seven States.* National Center for State Courts: Publication No. 50054.

10. See: Constitutional Jurisdiction of the Florida Supreme Court: 1980 Reform, in Powell, *Court Reform in Seven States.* Unfortunately, Chief Justice Englander does not explain what he means by good public policy.

11. A useful discussion of this topic may be found in: Tobin, Robert W., and Richard B. Hoffman. 1979. *The Administrative Role of Chief Justices and Supreme Courts.* National Center for State Courts: Publication No. 10046.

12. Terms of office ranged from six to fourteen years, to age 70, to life tenure. Age 70 was coded as 20 and life tenure was coded as 25.

13. The other variables which did not load high on the first factor were simply discarded. The loss of limited jurisdiction courts seems trivial, while the term of office is included to some extent in the first dimension, judicial recruitment plan. Term of office and selection system exhibit almost identical regional patterns and are related to each other. For example, the following relationships existed in 1976:

$$\text{Recruitment—Region, lambda} = 0.37, p = 0.00$$

$$\text{Term—Region, eta} = 0.46, p = 0.01$$

$$\text{Term—Recruitment, eta} = 0.26, p = 0.06$$

14. The median was chosen as the division point because it avoids the problem of deciding on an arbitrary standard which quickly becomes outdated. The result is, of course, only a relative ranking.

15. Alaska and Hawaii were not included in Elazar's 1966 study.

3. The Justices

This chapter examines the social and political backgrounds of state supreme court justices. The literature outlined in Chapter 1 suggests two important reasons for the study of judicial backgrounds: the representativeness of the judges of the diversity of the American population and the effect of social backgrounds on the development of attitudes which may influence decision-making on the bench. I would like to propose a third reason for the study of judicial backgrounds. I believe that the high degree of similarity in the backgrounds of state supreme court justices—as well as the standardization of career patterns—may be viewed in the light of Polsby's (1968) concept of "institutionalization" as applied to the state judiciary.[1]

THE DATA BASE

The data on the judicial backgrounds were drawn from the capsule biographies contained in *The American Bench* and *Who's Who*, while the data on formal recruitment were drawn from the 1976 and 1978 editions of *State Court Systems*, a publication of the Council on State Government. A total of 245 biographies were coded for 1975 and 270 for 1977. These figures represent 76.7 percent of all state court of last resort justices for the year 1975 and 82.8 percent for 1977. Each state supreme court is represented by at least two justices in both years. Please note that both Texas and Oklahoma have two courts of last resort, one committed to criminal appeals, the other to civil. This data set contains information for only the civil appeals courts for both states.

Of course, it can be argued (and this point is readily conceded) that a data set spanning only two years is insufficient to detect any real changes in the membership of the courts. Indeed, Table 3.1 indicates the extent of the similarity of the courts in 1975 and 1977. However, in a number of instances, the results obtained were only marginally statistically significant in one year; yet in the other, the significance vanishes. I believe the inclusion of both years helps to emphasize the fundamental similarity in the social backgrounds of the state court justices.

The multitude of formal judicial recruitment processes in the states reflects, in part, the states' efforts to balance the need for an independent judiciary with the desire for some degree of popular control of the "least dangerous branch" of government in a representative democracy. Some states have tipped this balance in favor of an independent judiciary. Therefore, these states have adopted formal judicial recruitment processes requiring appointed judges with long terms of office or life tenure. Other states have stressed the desire for popular control of the judiciary. The recruitment plans of these states provide for elected judges with relatively short, six- or eight-year, terms of office. Even the Missouri (or merit) Plan grew out of the judicial reform movement; it too embodies an effort to balance judicial independence and popular control by requiring the initial appointment of a judge from a limited list of qualified candidates and subsequent popular approval in a retention election on the judge's record. Consequently, I use the criterion of degree of popular control in collapsing categories of formal recruitment processes.[2]

A COLLECTIVE PORTRAIT

Table 3.1 summarizes the social backgrounds of the state supreme court justices for 1975 and 1977. Inspection of this table quickly reveals two things about these justices: there is substantial similarity in their backgrounds, and they are certainly not a representative sample of the people of the United States. On the whole, these jurists are white, male Protestants who were born in a small town in the same state as the court on which they will eventually serve. Most of them attended in-state colleges and law schools, and nearly half (48.1 percent in 1975 and 46.0 percent in 1977) were born and educated, both college and law school, in their native states. The majority has served in the armed forces, which is not surprising since most came of age during World War II. More than two-thirds have prior judicial experience. In fact, 43.0 percent in 1975 and 42.2 percent in 1977 came from primarily judicial careers. While a substantial percentage of the justices indicated supreme-court political activity, less than one-third held an elected office and less than 4 percent, in both 1975 and 1977, could be called career politicians. The justices of the state supreme courts come from primarily judicial or legal careers: they can scarcely be called "political hacks."

The lives of the state court justices follow similar pathways to the Supreme Court up until the choice of a profession. Typically, a justice is born, reared and educated in his or her native state, serves a stint in the military, usually as an officer, and returns home to begin to practice law either as a prosecutor or a private practice attorney. At this point in their lives they become involved in politics, working for a political party or spending a term or two in the state legislature. It is here, as well, that the path to the supreme court splits. Some of the future justices choose judicial careers, entering the lower state judiciary and serving, on the average, eleven years before being elevated to the state court of last resort. Other future justices choose primarily legal careers, remaining as prosecutors or private practice attorneys until taking a seat on the supreme court. It should be pointed out that there is only one statistically significant difference in the social backgrounds of the career judges and the career lawyers. The career judges tend to reach the supreme court later in life than the career lawyers. The average age of the career judges at the time of elevation to the supreme court is approximately fifty-three years, while the average for the career lawyers is about fifty years.[3]

It is important to note the similarities in the social backgrounds of career patterns. While judgeships are political offices, state supreme court justices are not professional politicians, although most have been involved politically at one time or another in their careers. Moreover, the political experience of the justices is particularly state and local in nature. Only the smallest fraction of future justices has some political experience at the national level. All of the justices, except one in 1975, have formal legal training, and more than two-thirds have prior judicial experience.[4] As a group, the justices average about seven years of judicial experience before the supreme court. If only those with judicial experience are considered, the average jumps to eleven years of court service. These findings lend support to the idea of the insti-

Table 3.1 All Justices: State Courts of Last Resort, 1975, 1977

Variable	1975 n=(245)		1977 n=(270)	
	n	Percent	n	Percent
Prior Judicial Experience	163	67.1%	175	65.1%
Sex				
Female	4	1.6	9	3.3
Male	241	98.3	261	96.7
Race				
White	241	99.6	263	98.1
Black	1	00.4	5	1.9
Previous Political Activity[1]	109	44.5	114	42.2
Political Party				
Democratic	77	72.6	92	74.2
Republican	27	25.5	30	24.2
Independent	2	1.9	2	1.6
Attended In-State College	157	72.4	174	71.0
Attended Ivy League College	23	10.6	27	11.0
Attended In-State Law School	163	67.4	174	65.2
Attended Ivy League Law School	38	15.7	47	17.6
Born In-State	191	80.3	204	77.9
Birthplace Size				
Urban	83	35.2	90	34.9
Small Town	141	59.7	154	59.7
Rural	12	5.1	14	5.4
Religion				
Protestant	134	74.0	139	71.3
Jewish	8	4.4	8	4.1
Catholic	33	18.2	39	20.0
Other	6	3.3	9	4.6
Additional Study[2]	28	11.4	32	11.9
Held Elected Political Office[3]	80	32.7	81	30.0
Prosecutorial Experience	113	46.1	121	44.8
Military Service	149	60.8	169	62.6
Served as Chief Justice	63	25.8	63	23.3

Table 3.1—Continued

Variable	1975 n=(245)		1977 n=(270)	
	n	Percent	n	Percent
(Primary) Pre-Supreme Court Career				
Law Professor	10	4.1	15	5.6
Judge	104	43.0	113	42.2
Practicing Attorney	88	36.4	95	35.4
Prosecutor	31	12.8	31	11.6
Elected Official	6	2.5	10	3.7
Other Politics	1	0.4	2	0.7
Business	1	0.4	1	0.4
Law Enforcement	0	0.0	0	0.0
Military	1	0.4	1	0.4
Religious Status[4]				
High Status Protestants	77	42.5	77	39.7
Low Status Protestants	55	30.4	58	29.9
Catholics and Jews	49	27.1	59	30.4
Localism[5]				
All In-State	101	48.1	111	46.6
		1975		1977
Average Years of Judicial Experience[6]		$\bar{X}=7.2$		$\bar{X}=7.0$
Average Years of Judicial Experience[7]		$\bar{X}=11.3$		$\bar{X}=11.0$
Age at Elevation to Supreme Court		$\bar{X}=51.9$		$\bar{X}=51.8$
Tenure on State Supreme Court (years)		$X'-=8.1$		$X'-=8.6$

NOTE: Discrepancies between N's and percents given are due to the exclusion of missing values. Percentages may not total 100% due to rounding error.

[1]Variable includes elected and appointed political offices as well as party activity. Lower court elected and appointed judgeships and elected and appointed legal posts (such as a district attorney) are excluded. Percentages are based upon the number of justices who indicated previous political activity in their biographical sketches. The actual percent of justices with previous political activity may be higher.

Table 3.1—Continued

²Variable includes any degree or formal training beyond the baccalaureate or law degree (J.D. or Ll.B.). The most common form of supplementary study is participation in appellate judges training seminars.

³Variable excludes elected judicial and legal positions (such as district attorney).

⁴"High Status" Protestants include: Episcopalians, Presbyterians, Congregationalists and Unitarians. This is the same classification used by Scmidhauser (1959).

⁵This figure represents the percentage of justices who were born and educated (college and law school) in the same state as the court on which they serve.

⁶Calculation of mean includes all justices, including those with no experience.

⁷Calculation of mean includes only those justices with prior judicial experience.

---

tutionalization of the state judiciary. The need for formal legal training makes membership in the state judiciary difficult. There is also commonly a period of apprenticeship in the lower courts of the state. Finally, the leadership of the state judiciary—the state supreme court—is recruited from within the judiciary, the lower state courts.

The leadership of the state supreme courts, the chief justices, is not very different from the associate members of the courts. In only two instances are there statistically significant differences between the chief and the associate justices. A greater fraction of the chief justices were members of the Republican Party, and the chiefs averaged 11.0 years on the supreme court in 1975 and 12.3 years in 1977, as compared to 6.9 and 7.4 years, respectively, for the associates. However, the difference in tenure on the supreme court is readily accounted for by the way in which a number of states choose their chief justices. In both 1975 and 1977, seven state supreme courts chose their chief justices by seniority of service on the court, while another four supreme courts selected the chief justice by awarding the leadership position to the justice with the shortest period of time remaining in his or her term. These eleven state procedures bias the average length of service on the court in favor of the chief justice. I believe that the difference in tenure between chief and associate justices is simply an artifact of the selection procedures for chief justice.

RECRUITMENT AND JUDICIAL BACKGROUNDS

A crude way by which to distinguish justices is whether they came to the supreme court through election or appointment. For the purposes of this basic comparison, elected justices are all those chosen through partisan, nonpartisan or legislative election, while appointed judges are selected through the formal processes of gubernatorial appointment, Missouri Plan or the informal process of interim appointment. There is one marginally significant difference between elected and appointed justices: the holding of an elected office before coming to the supreme court. A larger fraction of elected judges once held other elected political offices. In no other instance is the difference statistically significant.

The results presented in Table A.2 (see appendix) reflect the social backgrounds of the justices by the state's formal recruitment process. I have identified four basic recruitment processes:

1. appointment—gubernatorial appointment with or without the benefit of a merit list of qualified candidates
2. mixed system—the Missouri Plan or a variation thereof in which there is initial appointment with the requirement of a subsequent retention election based on the judge's record
3. nonpartisan election—popular election without party labels on the ballot
4. partisan election—popular election with party labels (includes legislative election states)

It is necessary to collapse the different formal recruitment processes into as few categories as possible to avoid the problem of expected cell frequencies of less than five in the calculation of the chi-square value for the test of statistical significance. Tables which contain cells with expected frequencies of less than five violate the assumption of continuity in the distribution of chi-square values. Therefore, significance levels tend to be inflated, and interpretation of results becomes difficult.[5]

At first there appear to be a number of statistically significant differences in the justices when they are divided by formal recruitment process. Justices of the majority Democratic Party are more often found in elected courts. The highest proportion of locally educated justices is found in elected courts, while the highest proportion of justices educated in Ivy League schools is found in the appointed states. Mixed systems states have the highest percentage of justices with prosecutorial experience, and partisan and nonpartisan election supreme courts are dominated by justices born and educated in their native states. There are also statistically significant differences in religious affiliation and religious status. The greatest fractions of non-Protestants are found in appointed and nonpartisan election states, and "low status" Protestants prevail in partisan election states. The reader is referred to Table A.2 to review these results.

However, all these relationships become statistically insignificant when controls for geographic region are introduced. The results reported in Table A.2 actually reflect regional variation in judicial backgrounds. This result is not surprising and is a consequence of the well-known relationship between region and formal judicial recruitment plans (see, for example, Canon, 1971; Glenn R. Winters and Robert E. Allard, 1965). Table A.3 (see appendix) summarizes the regional patterns in judicial backgrounds. In general, northern justices are more likely to be born in an urban area and attend Ivy League schools. This result is hardly surprising, given the population density of the northeast and the location of Ivy League institutions. The North also has the greatest percentage of non-Protestant judges and the smallest percentage of justices born and educated in the same state. Also, northern justices tend to be older and career jurists. Southern justices, on the other hand, are more likely to be smalltown residents and completely the products of local education. They are Democrats and, usually, "low status" Protestants. Southern justices are for the most part, career lawyers, and southern courts have the highest percentage of members with no previous judicial experience. Interestingly, northern and southern justices have similar levels of previous political activity.

The justices of the Midwest are second to the justices of the South in localism and incidence of smalltown birth. Midwestern justices rank just after their colleagues in the North in the proportion of career judges and justices with some previous judicial experience. There is one unique feature of the justices of the supreme courts of the Midwest: here, there are more Republicans than Democrats. Finally, more than half the midwestern justices have had some prosecutorial experience. The justices of the West resemble their colleagues in the North in their incidence of localism, non-Protestants and attendance at Ivy League institutions. However, western courts have the lowest proportion of career judges and the highest proportion of career prosecutors. The West and Midwest are similar in the percentage of justices with pre-supreme court political experience.

There are only two cases in which formal recruitment exhibits independent effects on judicial backgrounds, and both cases are limited to the South. Here, the mixed and appointed systems succeed in bringing more Republicans and Ivy Leaguers to the high bench. However, these results should be interpreted with caution due to the problems associated with the analysis of small marginals.

These results seem to indicate that regional variation in judicial backgrounds probably reflects local political culture rather than the effects of the operation of formal judicial recruitment plans. Within each geographical region, different methods of formal recruitment do not succeed in bringing different kinds of individuals to the supreme court. This finding is consistent with the idea of an institutionalized state judiciary in which career patterns and backgrounds become standardized. However, formal judicial recruitment plans should not be looked upon as failures because they fail to bring individuals of different backgrounds to the bench. Instead, the variations in formal judicial recruitment should be looked upon as different means to the same end: a professional, stable state judiciary. Each plan, within each geographic region and with only minor exceptions, functions to recruit legal professionals who are, in more than two-thirds of the cases, experienced judges.

Some scholars have argued that the lack of a relationship between formal recruitment and judicial backgrounds can be accounted for by the way in which interim appointments can undermine the formal process (Atkins and Glick, 1974; Canon, 1972). This is an interesting point especially considering that 27.3 percent of the justices in 1975 and 25.7 percent in 1977 were initially seated on the courts by interim appointment. A comparison of interim appointees with all formally recruited justices (see Table A.4 in the appendix) shows few statistically significant differences in judicial backgrounds once controls are introduced for the confounding effects of region. In the South, interim appointees are more likely to be from small towns and rural areas than formally recruited justices. In the North, interim appointees have a higher incidence of prosecutorial experience than their formally recruited counterparts. There is a slight suggestion in the data that interim appointees are safe, acceptable political choices and that a more diverse bench (to the extent that the benches of the state supreme court can be called diverse) results from the operation of the formal process. For example, interim appointees have a lower degree of judicial experience, are slightly older and more likely to be local products, Democrats and Protestant than the formally recruited justices. The interim appointees are also more likely to have prosecutorial experience. However, none of these results is statistically significant, and, again, the most remarkable finding is the degree of similarity. However, these differences, although slight, may furnish some grounds on which to argue for the restriction of interim appointments.

The introduction of a merit element to formal judicial recruitment was heralded by court reformers and the American Bar Association as an important means by which to assure the placement of only qualified individuals in a state's courts. (See, for example, Watson and Downing, 1969; Winters and Allard, 1965). However, in my examination of judicial backgrounds, I have detected virtually no difference between state supreme court justices selected via merit plan and those justices who came to the bench without the benefit of approval by a judicial qualifications committee. Like the case of interim appointment, there are only two instances in which the use of a merit plan had any statistically significant relationship to judicial backgrounds once a regional control was introduced. The operation of merit plans in the Midwest helped to increase the percent of Republicans serving the courts, but this relationship was significant in 1977 only. In the South, and again in only 1977, the merit plan succeeded in increasing the fraction of justices with prosecutorial experience. Critics of merit plans have argued that the plans will not increase the quality of state judges but will simply strengthen the hold of the American Bar Association and sitting judges on state judicial positions. If these critics are correct, we should expect to see the benches of merit plan states dominated by career judges. However, this data set reveals virtually the same proportion of career judges in merit plan and non-merit plan states. In fact, in 1977, the non-merit plan states had a higher percentage of career judges on the supreme court than merit plan states. The argument that merit plans will add some special contribution to the establishment of a judicial aristocracy in the United States appears to be unfounded.

JUDICIAL BACKGROUNDS AND TERMS OF OFFICE

The promise of life tenure to a judge is made to allow the judge to render unpopular decisions in the interest of justice without fear of jeopardizing his or her career. This freedom to do the "right," rather than the expedient, thing should provide a strong incentive for civic-minded individuals to engage in public service in the state judiciary. However, only one state, Rhode Island, offers life tenure to its supreme court justices, although a few others (Massachusetts, New Hampshire and New Jersey) allow a justice to serve an unlimited term up until mandatory retirement at age 70.[6] The dominant pattern in the states is specified terms of office for judges and justices, ranging from six years in sixteen states to fourteen years in New York. Therefore, to assess the impact of term of office on judicial backgrounds, I have divided the state courts into two categories by length of the term of office for the supreme court. "Short term" courts have six- to eight-year terms of office, while "long term" courts offer ten-year terms to life tenure. Hypothetically, long term court should be more successful than short term court in attracting exceptional legal talent (measured by Ivy League education) and public-spirited individuals (measured by pre-court political experience) to the bench. This theory is grounded in the belief that increased job security will allow justices to accept the challenge of making hard choices without fear of retaliation at the polls in the next judicial election.

These hypotheses hold to a limited degree in only two geographic regions of the United States. In the south, the promise of a long term of office helped bring more politically experienced lawyers to the supreme court in both 1975 and 1977. In 1977, seventeen (77.3 percent) of the long term justices indicated some pre-court political experience, while only twenty-six (39.4 percent) of the short term justices made the same claim. The difference is statistically significant at the 0.001 level as measured by the chi-square test. Similar, but less dramatic, differences were seen in 1975 when eighteen (75.0 percent) of the long term justices, as compared to twenty-nine (43.3 percent) of the short term justices claimed some pre-court political experience. This difference was statistically significant at the 0.015 level. Long terms in the South also helped to lure graduates of Ivy League universities to the supreme courts. Graduates of Ivy League universities appear only on long term courts, but these results are not statistically significant because only four southern justices (for a grand total of 5.0 percent) ever attended any of the prestigious East Coast schools. Long terms of office apparently made a significant difference on the presence of Ivy League law school graduates on the benches of western supreme courts in 1975 and 1977. Eight of the long term court justices (40.0 percent) trained at Ivy League institutions, while only a single short term justice (2.8 percent) received a similar education. These results are significant at the 0.001 level and are identical to the findings for 1975.

JUDICIAL BACKGROUNDS AND THE COURT CLASSIFICATIONS

In Chapter 2, I developed a classification system for state courts of last resort that groups courts along two dimensions, yielding a sixfold typology. In the next few paragraphs, I test the ability of the classification system to distinguish among the justices from the different courts.[7]

The division of the justices by the court classification system reveals differences in education and localism among the justices. The justices of Class II, Class III and Class VI states are most likely to be educated in-state and score the highest on the localism scale. More than 83 percent of the Class II and Class III justices attended an in-state college, while almost 78 percent of the Class VI justices were similarly educated in 1975 and 1977. The justices of the Class II, Class III and Class VI courts also possess the most parochial backgrounds. In 1975 and 1977, approximately 59 percent of the Class II justices, 58 percent of the Class III justices, and 57 percent of the Class VI justices were born and educated, both college and law school, in the state on whose court they will eventually serve. The justices of these court classes also exhibit the lowest incidence of Ivy League college education. None of the Class II justices attended an Ivy League college, while only 7 percent of the Class III justices and 6 percent of the Class VI justices had the privilege of attending one of these old, prestigious schools. Class II and Class III courts have the fewest number of justices with Ivy League legal training: 4 percent of the Class II justices and 7 percent of the Class III justices attended an Ivy League law school. Class IV courts do not do as badly in attracting Ivy League lawyers to their benches: 19 percent of all Class VI justices had such legal education. In the category of Ivy League legal training, Class V justices rank after their Class II and Class III colleagues. Only 15 percent of the Class V justices attended an Ivy League law school.

The justices of the Class V states are relatively undistinguished. Generally, these justices rank about fourth among the court classes with respect to the incidence of in-state education, Ivy League education and localism. Of the Class V justices, 60 percent attended an in-state college and 59 percent an in-state law school. Thirty-six percent of these justices are completely local products, ranking after Class II, Class III, and Class VI on the localism scale. The Class V justices also rank fourth in the fraction of justices (15 percent) who were educated at Ivy League law schools. Only in the category of Ivy League college education do the Class V justices rise above their customary fourth position: 16 percent of Class V justices were educated at an Ivy League college, the third highest proportion among the six court classes.

The Class I and Class IV courts are characterized by a high proportion of justices who are Ivy League graduates. Thirty-three percent of the Class I justices attended an Ivy League college, the largest fraction among the court classes, and 24 percent attended an Ivy League law school, the second highest figure. The Class IV justices rank just after their Class I counterparts with respect to Ivy League college education (23 percent) and replace the Class I justices as first among the court classes in Ivy League legal training (44 percent). The Class I and Class IV justices also rank lowest on the localism scale. Only 17 percent of the Class I justices and 15 percent of the Class IV justices were born and entirely educated within the state on whose court they will eventually serve.

The model of some factors related to state supreme court performance proposed in Chapter 1 indicates that the institutional characteristics of the state judiciary should have an impact on the social backgrounds of the justices. Social backgrounds, in turn, should influence a justice's attitudes and perception of the judicial role. These variables, then, should be linked to various measures of supreme court performance. In this chapter, I have focused on the relationship between institutional characteristics—formal recruitment and term of office—and judicial backgrounds and found very few statistically significant effects. Variations in formal recruitment processes, despite all the arguments of the partisans of the different plans, seem to make no difference in the social backgrounds of the justices once regional controls are introduced. Any apparent difference in the social backgrounds of the justices is, in reality, a product of regional differences rather than the result of the operation of the formal recruitment process. The effects of region and recruitment on social backgrounds are complicated by the relationship between region (or political culture) and recruitment processes as seen in Chapter 2. The net result, however, is that formal recruitment processes, whatever they may be, are remarkably successful in bringing similar individuals who followed similar career patterns to the benches of the state supreme courts.

This phenomenon, in my view, should not be looked upon as an indication of the failure of formal recruitment in the states. Instead, this is an example of what Polsby (1968) has called "institutionalization." According to Polsby, when an organization has achieved a certain critical mass of work to be performed, it must develop stable recruitment patterns and internal procedures in order for it to survive to perform its required tasks. I believe the standardization of social backgrounds and pre-court career patterns should be seen as an element of the institutionalization of the state judiciary. Given the immense caseload of many state supreme courts, particularly those with little discretion in choosing cases for review or without the assistance of an intermediate appellate court, it is necessary for the efficient processing of cases to staff the courts with professional justices who are familiar with the needs of the state judiciary. The formal recruitment processes in the states seem to have succeeded in securing such legal professionals. The state supreme court justices are local products and, in the large majority of cases, career state judges, attorneys or prosecutors. Therefore, they are familiar with the inner workings and problems of the state court system. Moreover, the majority of state supreme court justices are career judges who have worked their way up through the levels of the state judiciary. In this sense, many state supreme court justices are professional state judges—individuals who have geared their career choices to secure a place on the state bench. Perhaps American judges have created for themselves a de facto system of professional judicial education similar to some of their European counterparts who undergo specialized training to become judges. In any event, the standardization of career patterns—or institutionalization—is a necessary element in the stability and efficient function of the state judiciary.

Despite the apparent success of formal recruitment plans in securing qualified legal professionals for the state supreme courts, I do not believe the plans are of equal value. Career patterns and social backgrounds tell us nothing about an individual's conception of the judicial role. There are a number of important questions students of state courts and federalism, or anyone else interested in the policymaking role of the supreme courts, would like to address to candidates for a position on the court. Some questions would pertain to the classic debate over the law-maker/law interpreter conception of the judicial role. Other questions would probe the individual's feelings on the proper relationship between a state supreme court and the United States Supreme Court or between state constitutional guarantees of civil rights and liberties and the federal Bill of Rights. Not all methods of formal recruitment provide the same opportunities to ask these questions. Partisan elections may provide some chance to ask these questions of potential justices at the nominating convention, but the primary focus at a party nominating convention is identifying candidates who can win. True nonpartisan election of justices is dependent on self-nomination and the development of a personal electoral coalition to secure candidates for judicial office. Here, I would suggest that personality and "contacts" are more important to the campaign than conception of the judicial role. Voters in low salience judicial elections work with minimal information—party label, name recognition, ethnic affiliation—and cannot be relied upon to consider such obscure and esoteric issues such as whether or not the federal Bill of Rights should be regarded as providing minimal standards for the protection of civil liberties. Moreover, the Canons of Judicial Ethics precludes candidates for judicial office from making campaign statements on future behavior on the bench.[8] Thus judicial campaigns become simple quests for name recognition or a presentation of a litany of credentials. However, appointed systems, whether or not they include a merit element or retention election, provide the opportunity for an interested governor or state legislature to ask sophisticated and important questions of judicial nominees. For those interested in the development of an independent and adequate state law for the protection of civil liberties, or the policymaking role of the state judiciary, appointed systems are preferable over elected systems to the extent to which appointed systems provide the opportunity for an investigation of the philosophy of the candidates.

NOTES

1. It should be noted that one researcher has found Polsby's indices of institutionalization of limited utility in assessing professionalism in two state legislatures. See: Chaffey, Douglas C. 1970. The Institutionalization of State Legislatures: A Comparative Study. *Western Political Quarterly*, 23:180–96. However, even Chaffey concedes the importance of the concept.

2. Selection by legislative election is problematic here because, while the justices are elected, they are elected by an elite body. I have chosen to treat legislative election as closest to partisan election.

3. The statistical significance of the difference between the means was determined through T-tests. For both years, the difference was significant at better than 0.01.

4. Some states have no legal requirement of formal legal training for judges, but it is virtually impossible for a non-lawyer to be chosen for anything but a position at the lowest rungs of the judicial hierarchy.

5. For a detailed discussion of this phenomenon, see: Blalock, Herbert M., Jr. 1972. *Social Statistics*, 2d ed. New York: McGraw-Hill, especially Chapter 15.

6. New Jersey Supreme Court justices actually serve an initial seven-year term with reappointment, after the seventh year, to age 70.

7. The figures listed in the following discussions are drawn from the results for the 1975 courts. These percentages are substantially unchanged for 1977.

8. Canon 7B (1)(c) requires that: "A candidate, including an incumbent judge, for judicial office that is filled either by public election between competing candidates or on the basis of a merit system election should not make pledge or promises of conduct in office other than the faithful and impartial performance of the duties of office; announce his views on disputed legal or political issues; or misrepresent his identity, qualification, present position or other fact."

4. The Work of Six Supreme Courts

In this chapter, I compare the performance of six state courts of last resort—Arizona, Kentucky, California, Michigan, Nebraska and New Jersey—for 1975. I focus on three measures of performance: dissent rates, rates of reversals of lower court decisions and judicial activism scores. I also formulate some theories to account for the variation in the performance of the courts.

METHODOLOGY

The opinions of six state courts of last resort for 1975 were content analyzed and coded in the effort to illustrate some aspects of the model of state court performance presented in Chapter 1. I have selected one state from each of the six court classes for study. The state courts chosen exhibit different institutional and cultural characteristics, but I make no attempt to argue that this limited sample of courts is representative of all the states. Therefore, I do not argue that my findings here are generalizable to all state courts of last resort. However, I do believe my findings are suggestive since they seem to point to fruitful areas for future, comprehensive studies.

I have chosen to begin my study of state supreme courts in 1975. This choice was based upon practical and theoretical reasons. The 1976 edition of *State Court Systems,* which describes the institutional characteristics of the state courts just prior to January 1, 1976, is the first readily available catalogue of information on the courts of all fifty states. Since I am interested in the effect of institutional characteristics on state supreme court performance, my choice of years for the study was limited to those years for which the *State Court Systems* data were available. More importantly, 1975 marks the outset of serious discussion of the "new judicial federalism," with its emphasis on greater responsibility for state supreme courts. By 1975, the so-called Nixon Court had already established a commitment to a crime control, rather than due process, philosophy and had embarked upon a course of gradual erosion of the liberal Warren Court decisions, particularly in cases concerning the Fourth and Fifth Amendments. This conservative posture of the United States Supreme Court prompted civil libertarians to begin to consider the use of state courts and constitutions for the vindication of individual rights. By 1975, Chief Justice Burger had also indicated his concern over the ever-increasing docket of the federal Court. Therefore, he urged state courts to begin to assume increased responsibility for constitutional adjudication in order to decrease the workload of the federal courts. The appearance of this new emphasis on the role of state courts makes 1975 a reasonable choice for a base year in which to begin the systematic study of state court performance. The judicial year for this study begins on January 1, 1975, and ends on December 31, 1975.

All cases, except memorandum opinions and orders, were coded for all six courts, including the panel decisions of the Arizona and Nebraska supreme courts. This procedure gives an N of 212 cases for Arizona (of which 170 were decided en banc and 42 in division), 166 for California, 170 for Kentucky, 112 for Michigan, 362 for Nebraska (280 en banc, 82 in division) and 103 for New Jersey, for a total of 1,125 cases. The following information was coded for each of the opinions:

1. Did the court reverse the decision of the lower court?
2. Did the court grant the writ, if any (e.g., habeas corpus, mandamus, prohibition, etc.), requested by the appellant?
3. Was the decision unanimous?
4. How many dissenting and/or concurring opinions were filed?
5. What was the vote of the justices?
6. What issues were presented by the case?
7. What sister state precedents were cited by the court?
8. What law review or other scholarly articles were cited?

9. Did the case involve judicial review?
10. Were independent and adequate state grounds invoked?

Up to three sister state precedents and three law review citations were coded in the order in which they appeared in the majority or plurality opinion. A similar procedure was followed for the issues presented in the case: up to three issues were coded in the order in which they appeared in the majority or plurality opinion. I believe the use of multiple responses helps to capture the complexity of the cases considered by the state supreme courts. However, this choice of multiple responses involves an important trade-off because the use of multiple responses makes it impossible to identify a case as purely "constitutional" or "statutory," or "federal" or "state" in nature. Therefore, none of the crosstabulation tables presented contains an unidimensional case. For example, a case will be considered "constitutional" if any of the three coded issues embodies a constitutional question. I believe the use of multiple responses helps this research overcome the problem contained in other comparative studies of treating any given case as presenting a single question of law.[1] The nature of this problem is best illustrated through an example. In 1975, the courts of last resort of California, Michigan and Nebraska considered a series of cases which ultimately involved challenges to the constitutionality of automobile guest passenger statutes. These challenges originated in what originally appeared to be simple automobile collision cases. However, the trial courts in each state had to consider the limits on recovery of damages by passengers against the drivers posed by the state's guest passenger statute. Ultimately, the courts of last resort considered the issues of negligence, the interpretation of legislative intent behind guest passenger statutes and the constitutionality of the statutes under federal and state due process and equal protection clauses. Are these cases private tort actions? Are these cases examples of statutory interpretation? Or are these constitutional cases and, if so, which constitution? A unidimensional approach to the classification of cases would force the researcher to choose among three arguably correct alternatives. However, the use of multiple responses allows a researcher to avoid these judgment calls and thereby increase the reliability of the coding system and capture the complexity of the cases.

Another weakness of earlier comparative studies of state supreme courts is the use of overbroad categories by which to classify cases.

Kagan et al. (1978) developed a fourfold classification of cases while Atkins and Glick (1976) utilized a fivefold typology.[2] These classification systems also fail to distinguish between reliance on federal or state grounds, which is particularly problematic in assessing state court activism in the context of the new judicial federalism. To overcome these deficiencies, I have developed a detailed system for the classification of state courts cases, presented in Table A.5 (see appendix). Each issue considered in a case is assigned a three-digit code number. The first digit in the code represents the major issue area, and the second and third digits represent subdivisions of the major area. Codes 100 to 165 (the 100 Series) are subjects in the United States Constitution. For example, code 104 is Article I, section 8, the enumerated powers of Congress, and code 142 is the Sixth Amendment guarantee of the right to counsel. The 100 Series of codes is elaborate enough to distinguish between different provisions of an article or an amendment. Under this system, therefore, it is possible to distinguish among the equal protection, due process and privileges and immunities guarantees of the Fourteenth Amendment.

The 200 Series represents state constitutional provisions. Codes 200 to 265 are the state constitutional analogs to federal constitutional provisions. For example, code 204 indicates powers of the state legislature, while code 242 would be a state constitutional guarantee of the right to counsel in criminal proceedings. Codes 266 and 299 represent state constitutional guarantees with no precise federal counterpart. This six-state study goes as far as code 285, but the remaining code numbers may be used if additional state constitutional guarantees appear in later studies. The 300 Series is made up of state statutes which fall into three broad subcategories: general regulatory laws, criminal procedure and civil procedure. The classification system for state statutes, particularly the groupings of general regulatory laws, is derived from the California Code, which is a rational and comprehensive attempt to organize state law. The remaining two series are the 400 Series, common law, and the 500 Series, federal statutes. Distinguishing between common law issues and state statutory issues presented some difficulties, especially in instances in which state statutes were enacted to adopt and modify the common law or in instances of poor judicial craftsmanship. Therefore, I adopted the following decision-rule in coding common law and statutory issues: any principle of law cited without reference to a particular statutory provision was coded as common law.

The Work of Six Supreme Courts 69

After examining the distribution of responses under this detailed coding scheme, it was determined that the categories could be collapsed into nine subject areas without the loss of too much information:

1. federal constitution: articles
2. federal constitution: amendments
3. state constitution: scope of government authority
4. state constitution: individual rights
5. federal statutes
6. state statutes: regulation
7. state statutes: criminal procedure
8. state statutes: civil procedure
9. common law

The combined workload of the courts of last resort of the six states, as broken down by the nine subject areas listed above, is summarized in Figure 4.1.

In Chapter 1, I proposed a quantitative measure to assess levels of state court activism in the context of the new judicial federalism. By

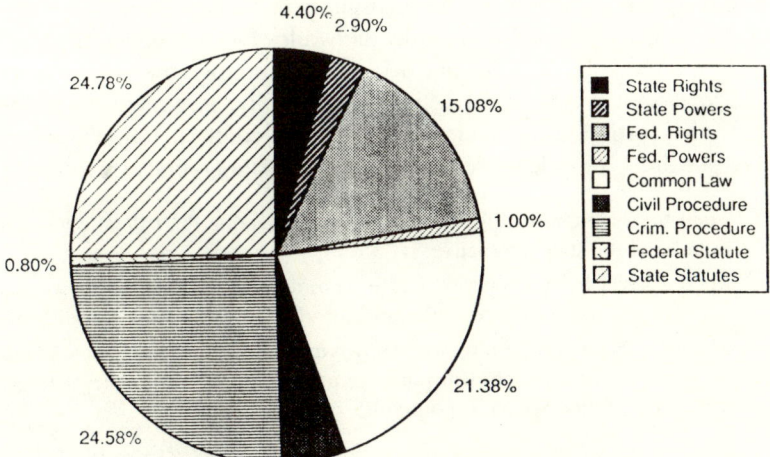

Figure 4.1 Issues in Six State Supreme Courts, 1975

the term "new judicial federalism," I generally mean state court development of an independent and adequate body of state constitutional law such that the states may be free to provide stricter protection for federally guaranteed rights and liberties, create new state-derived rights and liberties and tailor judicial decisions to the policy needs of the states. My measure of state court activism, therefore, focuses on the use of independent and adequate state grounds. However, coding for reliance on purely state grounds poses some important problems for the researcher because of the difficulty involved in determining just what exactly constitutes independent and adequate state grounds. Stanley H. Friedelbaum (1982: 23–24) states:

By judicial definition, the determination [of the presence of independent and adequate state grounds] in any case turns on the sufficiency of the state-law foundation on which the decision has been premised, the extent to which the non-federal question may be viewed as independent, and the degree to which the state-related issue or issues are capable of being maintained without "fair or substantial support" in federal law . . . [S]tate courts are free to accept or reject federal standards as long as the constitutional source is essentially state derived. Yet the state grounds set forth must be of sufficient cogency to sustain the judgment announced without any notable dependence on the federal question. Additionally, the state grounds must not be so intertwined with the federal grounds as to compromise the independence of the former.

Given the ambiguity in the definition of "independent" or "adequate," I have adopted narrow decision-rules for the coding of purely state grounds. These rules are designed to improve the reliability of this measure of state court activism. Generally, *any* mention of the federal Constitution or reference to a federal court citation *eliminates* the possibility of independent and adequate state grounds *except*:

1. when the state court explicitly declares it is rejecting the federal approach in favor of the state alternative
2. when a lower federal court is cited in common law or state statutory cases as a consequence of the federal court's exercise of its diversity jurisdiction
3. when the state court borrows well-known quotations from the United States Supreme Court for rhetorical purposes only (e.g., "We must never forget it is a constitution we are expounding."

This is a highly conservative approach to the coding of independent and adequate state grounds, and, consequently, there may be some slight loss of validity. In other words, the incidence of the use of purely state grounds may actually be somewhat higher than indicated in this research, but I believe this small loss of validity is more than compensated for by the increase in reliability. Moreover, the use of independent and adequate state grounds is but one element in an eight-point scale of judicial activism which also includes up to three law review citations and up to three citations of sister state precedents.

Finally, in the next chapter I discuss the "judicial professionalism score" of six state supreme courts. This score is derived from a scale based upon variables suggested by Schmidhauser (1979) to evaluate judicial independence and professionalism. A state court system is assigned one point for each constitutional or statutory requirement for judicial office (e.g., citizenship, minimum age, formal legal training, judicial experience); one point for scoring above the national median in salary for a supreme court justice; one point for the use of a merit element in formal judicial recruitment and one point for a term of office of ten years or longer. A point is deducted from the total score if the state provides for the recall of justices. The scores of the fifty state court systems ranged from a low of 3 to a high of 13, with a national mean of 8.0 and a national median of 8.2.

A COMPARISON OF THE PERFORMANCE OF SIX COURTS

Table 4.1 presents a comparison of the performance of six state courts of last resort—Arizona, California, Kentucky, Michigan, Nebraska and New Jersey—for 1975. It should be noted that this table and subsequent tables presented in this chapter contain only en banc decisions; the panel decision of the Arizona and Nebraska courts have been omitted. Furthermore, an asterisk placed beside a statistical significance level should be treated with care due to the presence of cells with expected frequencies of less than five in the calculation of the chi-square value.

Table 4.1 shows significant differences among the six state supreme courts. The Michigan Supreme Court was the court most likely to overturn the decision of the state's courts of appeal. In 58.3 percent of its decisions, the Michigan high court disagreed with the outcome of the lower court decision. At the other extreme with respect to reversal rates was the Nebraska Supreme Court, which overturned the

Table 4.1 All En Banc Cases

Variable	Arizona		California		Kentucky		Michigan		Nebraska		New Jersey		Significance[1]
	n	%	n	%	n	%	n	%	n	%	n	%	
Reverses Lower Court Decision	46	32.9	61	50.0	72	49.0	60	58.3	40	15.0	35	46.7	0.000
Unanimous Decisions	148	87.1	114	68.7	149	87.6	53	47.3	224	80.0	62	60.2	0.000
Full Dissenting Opinions Filed	10	5.9	35	21.1	13	7.6	37	33.0	29	10.4	23	22.3	0.000
Concurring Opinions Filed	10	5.9	13	7.8	3	1.8	19	17.0	9	3.2	17	16.5	0.000
Independent and Adequate State Grounds	81	47.6	122	67.5	149	87.6	88	78.6	221	78.9	76	73.8	0.000
Cases Decided Without Dissent	158	92.9	132	79.5	157	92.4	72	64.3	251	89.6	78	75.7	0.000
Judicial Activism Score													
(Least) 0	64	37.6	30	18.1	14	8.2	12	10.7	36	12.9	14	13.6	
1	69	40.6	78	47.0	128	75.3	64	57.1	163	65.4	54	52.4	
2	15	8.8	13	7.8	12	7.1	11	9.8	22	7.9	13	12.6	
3	13	7.6	20	12.0	7	4.1	13	11.6	21	7.5	7	6.8	0.000*
4	8	4.7	15	9.0	8	4.7	9	8.0	18	6.4	7	6.8	
5	1	0.6	3	1.8	0	0.0	2	1.8	0	0.0	5	4.9	
6	0	0.0	4	2.4	1	0.6	1	0.9	0	0.0	1	1.0	
(Most) 7	0	0.0	3	1.8	0	0.0	0	0.0	0	0.0	2	1.9	
Mean	1.03		1.71		1.24		1.58		1.29		1.69		
Examples of Judicial Review	2		9		1		5		1		3		
	n=170		n=166		n=170		n=112		n=280		n=103		Total=1001

[1]Significance levels marked by an asterisk should be treated with caution due to expected cell frequencies of five or less in the calculation of chi-square value.

decisions of lower courts 15.0 percent of the time. The Arizona court reversed the decisions of the intermediate appellate court 32.9 percent of the time, and the California, Kentucky and New Jersey courts had reversal rates which hovered at about 50 percent.

The differences in the reversal rates are difficult to explain. A possible theory is that supreme courts with intermediate appellate courts and substantial discretion in selection cases for review would exhibit the highest reversal rates. This theory is grounded in the belief that these supreme courts would be most likely to choose to review cases in which the justices believe the lower court has erred in the application of the law. The problematic cases are accepted for review, hence the high reversal rate. The supreme courts without the benefit of an intermediate appellate screening of cases and without much discretionary jurisdiction should show the lowest reversal rates. These courts are compelled to hear even the usual selection of frivolous appeals from the trial courts, and, because of the lack of merit in such appeals, it becomes easy to affirm summarily the decision of the trial court. Only two states here did not possess intermediate appellate courts in 1975: Nebraska and Kentucky. The Nebraska Supreme Court exhibits the low reversal rate that would be expected in a low-discretion, no-intermediate-appellate-court state. As will be seen in Chapter 5, the Nebraska court must hear all criminal appeals from the trial courts. A large fraction of these appeals was requests by prisoners for sentence review, and all except one were found without merit. In case after case, the supreme court simply rubber-stamped approval of any sentence imposed by the trial judge within the broad statutory limits. Unfortunately, the Kentucky Court of Appeals does not fit the theory. The Kentucky court had higher reversal rates than the New Jersey and Arizona courts, both of which had the benefit of an intermediate appellate screening of cases. However, I am reluctant to discard this theory on the basis of this limited sample. Complete testing of this theory, like countless others in science and social science, awaits further testing.

Another explanation for the variations in reversal rates could be the internal unity of the state. As discussed at greater length in Chapter 1, Elazar (1966) has argued that the states differ in their internal levels of agreement on cultural and political norms. I believe states with the highest levels of intrastate cohesiveness show the lowest reversal rates because most political actors, including trial and appellate judges, agree on the tacit rules which govern political decisions. Conversely, states with the lowest levels of intrastate cohesiveness show the highest reversal rates. Under Elazar's scoring system for state internal unity, Michigan scores eleven, indicating extremely low internal unity.[3] The Michigan Supreme Court also exhibited the highest reversal rate of the six courts under consideration here. Arizona rates highest in internal unity, and its supreme court showed the second lowest reversal rates. California and New Jersey have identical internal unity scores, and their respective courts of last resort exhibit similar reversal rates. Nebraska and Kentucky present problems for this theory. While the two states have the same internal unity scores, their highest courts have very different reversal rates. The imperfect fit between internal unity and reversals may be due to inaccuracies in Elazar's subjective rankings of internal unity or the inadequacy of the theory. As before, confirmation or rejection of the theory awaits further research.

While reversal rates are indicative of the extent of disagreement between a court of last resort and the lower appellate or trial courts, the proportion of unanimous decisions filed and levels of dissent and concurrence can be regarded as measures of disagreement among the justices of a supreme court. The most striking finding concerning disagreement on state supreme courts is its usual absence. In two states, Arizona and Kentucky, more than 92 percent of all decisions were reached without a single dissenting opinion, and more than 87 percent of the decisions of these courts were unanimous. The Nebraska Supreme Court also was relatively successful at achieving consensus among the justices: 80 percent of the Nebraska decisions were unanimous, and nearly 90 percent were decided without dissenting opinions. The California and New Jersey courts showed less agreement among the justices, but dissents were still uncommon. Although only 68.7 percent of the California decisions and 60.2 percent of the New Jersey decisions were unanimous, more than 75 percent of the decisions of both courts were reached without dissent. The Michigan Supreme Court was the most divided court under consideration. Less than half of its decisions were unanimous, and just more than two-thirds of the decisions were reached without dissent. The filing of concurring opinions appears to be an unusual practice among the justices of the state supreme courts. In 1975, concurrences were filed approximately 17 percent of the time in Michigan and New Jersey, while the concurrence rate in the other four courts was always less than 8 percent.

A number of theories have been advanced to explain dissenting behavior on state supreme courts. Jaros and Canon (1971) have suggested that states high in socioeconomic diversity and political competition tend to have supreme courts with relatively high dissent rates. These researchers also postulated that the presence of an intermediate appellate court in the state's judicial system, as well as the social backgrounds of the justices of the supreme court, contribute to variations in dissent rates. I would add state internal unity to the list of factors which can contribute to dissent rates. Other researchers have also theorized that social backgrounds, particularly political party affiliation, have an impact on dissents on state supreme courts (David W. Adamany, 1969; Ulmer, 1966, 1962). The Michigan Supreme Court has been especially well studied in this regard because, although Michigan Supreme Court justices are technically elected on a nonpartisan ballot, the parties openly nominate and endorse candidates. Moreover, the voting behavior of Democratic and Republican justices closely parallels the classic labor–business division in Michigan. My data on the Michigan court does not allow me to correlate social backgrounds with decisions, but my impression is that the high dissent rate is a function of the policy differences between Democratic and Republican justices.

I do not doubt that socioeconomic diversity, intermediate appellate courts and judicial backgrounds all play a part in the explanation of dissent rates. I would like to propose an additional factor which may account for the presence of supplementary opinions filed in the state supreme courts—the "maverick justice" theory. In two states, New Jersey and Nebraska, a disproportionate number of dissents and concurrences were written by two justices. Hale McCown of Nebraska and Morris Pashman of New Jersey felt compelled to write more supplementary opinions than any of their colleagues. Particularly in the case of the concurrences of Justice Pashman, these extra opinions did little to clarify the majority's position or develop a significantly different line of legal reasoning. I do not know what accounts for the independent personality of these justices: I will leave such speculation to mind readers and armchair psychologists. However, I do believe that the occasional presence of the random maverick justice should be considered along with other, more systematic explanations of opinion writing behavior.

Finally, the lack of dissent on state supreme courts should not necessarily be construed to connote a lack of disagreement among the justices. Robert J. Sickels (1965) has studied zoning decisions on the Maryland Court of Appeals and discovered that, while most of the decisions were unanimous, the outcome of the cases followed no predictable pattern. He concluded that unanimity did not reflect agreement among the justices. Instead, the unanimous result was actually a reflection of the justices' tendency to "logroll," that is, to cooperate with each other in voting for mutual benefit. I would like to suggest that logrolling may be a decision-making norm for some state supreme courts.

Richard F. Fenno, Jr. (1973), in his classic study of committees in the United States House of Representatives, noted how voting behavior of members of constituent service committees was governed by the norm of reciprocity which led members to logroll in order to maximize the chance of passage of all member-sponsored bills. It may be the case that different supreme courts may be governed by different decision-making norms. While there may be some danger in applying legislative studies to the judiciary, I believe Fenno's identification of decision norms in House committees may be of value in explaining dissents and concurrences by state supreme court justices. For example, the 1975 decisions of the Kentucky Court of Appeals show a genuine reluctance on the part of the justices to dissent or concur. Any dissenting or concurring opinion was usually prefaced by an apology for the author's need to disagree with some aspect of the wisdom of his brethren. It is conceivable that the decision-making process of the Kentucky court is governed by the norm of consensus whenever possible, much as the case of constituent service committees. Decision-making on the Michigan Supreme Court seems to approximate the behavior of Fenno's policy committees. For Fenno, all decisions in policy committees, such as Education and Labor, are ideologically charged throughout the committee's deliberations. Because of the partisan nature of the debate on these committees, members realize that the achievement of consensus on a given issue is probably impossible. Consequently, decision-making is governed by a norm that requires members simply to agree to disagree. The justices of the Michigan court seemed to operate by a similar norm. Unlike their Kentucky colleagues, Michigan justices showed no regret in penning sharply worded dissents from the majority. Numerous examples of this phenomenon can be found in any of the 1975 cases which featured a debate between Democratic Justice G. Mennen "Soapy" Williams, a former governor of Michigan, and Republican Justice Mary Stallings Coleman. Michigan justices seem to accept the partisan nature of their decisions and, like members of a House policy committee, make little or no effort to secure consensus.

The New Jersey and California courts may approximate Fenno's model of decision-making of members of House "power" committees, such as Appropriations or Ways and Means. Power committee members seek to maximize their prestige and influence within the House. Therefore, they seek to present a unified front to the parent chamber in order to increase the chances for bills to be passed without amendment from the floor. However, the members also recognize that their decision will necessarily involve highly ideological and partisan debate. To reconcile the partisan nature of the debate surrounding the work of power committees and its concomitant division with the desire for unanimity as the bills are presented to the House, power committee members will agree to disagree when the bills are deliberated in committee but further agree to try to put aside member differences when facing the House. The justices of the New Jersey and California courts may abide by a similar decision-making norm. The California and New Jersey courts are regarded as among the best policy-oriented supreme courts. The prestige and effectiveness of these courts may rest, in part, upon the justices' ability to present clear statements of the requirements of the law, unsullied by concurrences or dissents.[4] Of course, there was disagreement among the California and New Jersey justices, as seen in Table 4.1, but the levels of disagreement did not approach the level of the chronically divided Michigan court. My theories as to the operation of the different decision-making norms to explain dissent are based on personal impressions from a limited sample. Verification of the existence of such norms will require interviews with the justices of the state supreme courts.

Just as the six supreme courts differed in reversal rates and levels of disagreement among the justices, the courts also differ in levels of judicial activism. The courts of last resort of Kentucky and Nebraska showed the largest fraction of cases decided using independent and adequate state grounds, while the courts of Arizona and California invoked purely state law for decisions the least amount of times (see Table 4.1). These rather unexpected findings are easily explained. The Kentucky Court of Appeals handled a large fraction of common law and state statutory cases, particularly workmen's compensation. Since only 13.5 percent of all Kentucky cases included a constitutional issue, it was easy for the court to avoid resorting to federal grounds in a decision.[5] The situation was identical for the Nebraska Supreme Court: only 16.6 percent of all decisions embodied a constitutional claim. The poor showing of the Arizona Supreme Court in the use of independent and adequate state grounds is also a function of the nature of its docket. As will be seen in Chapter 5, the Arizona court is overwhelmed with petitions to review criminal cases, most of which arose from the smuggling of contraband from Mexico. Just more than 30 percent of all issues raised in Arizona were constitutional claims. A disproportionate number of these claims (11.8 percent of cases) involved searches and seizures. The justices of the Arizona court found the Burger Court's crime control approach to the Fourth Amendment suitable to the needs of Arizona. Consequently, there was no need to resort to innovative or independent interpretations of the Arizona constitution. The California Supreme Court considered more constitutional claims (35.3 percent) than any other court, and its decisions frequently made reference to the dual protection of individual rights available under the state and federal constitutions. The tendency for the California court to cite both constitutions accounts for the relatively low percentage of cases decided on independent and adequate state grounds. The large fraction of constitutional claims considered in the New Jersey (23.2 percent) and Michigan (22.4 percent) courts also accounts for the low frequency of use of independent and adequate state grounds.

Two more revealing indicators of the relative activism of the six state supreme courts are the judicial activism scores and the number of examples of judicial review. The overall judicial activism score ranks the courts in the following order from most to least activist: California, New Jersey, Michigan, Nebraska, Kentucky and Arizona. California, followed by Michigan, New Jersey and Arizona, leads the courts in the number of declarations of unconstitutionality, while Kentucky and Nebraska tied for last place.

Patterns for reversal rates, levels of intracourt disagreement and judicial activism remain the same if only state statutory cases are examined. These results are presented in Table A.6 (see appendix). As in the previous analysis of the entire docket of the courts, all of the differences among the courts are statistically significant. And, once again,

California, New Jersey and Michigan proved to have the most activist courts on the eight-point scale of judicial activism.

State supreme court activism reached its highest levels in common law cases. Table A.7 (see appendix) represents the relative performance of the six courts in all en banc decisions in which a common law issue was present. All state courts with the single exception of Nebraska scored higher in judicial activism in common law cases than any other issue area. Again, California, New Jersey and Michigan remained the most activist among the courts, and again all the differences among the courts are statistically significant. Michigan remained the most quarrelsome of the courts. Only 52.4 percent of all the Michigan common law cases were unanimous, although 69.0 percent of the decisions were reached without a full dissenting opinion.

The increase in judicial activism in common law cases is not surprising. Pure common law cases are decided without reference to either the federal or state constitutions; therefore, most of the cases were decided on the basis of independent and adequate state grounds. For example, 98.3 percent of the Kentucky cases and 92.3 percent of the California common law cases rested exclusively on state law. Arizona, with only 45.8 percent of cases, was the only state in which less than three-quarters of the decisions relied on independent and adequate state grounds. Moreover, the development of the common law is a traditional area of responsibility for the state courts. State supreme court justices probably feel more comfortable with innovation in common law than they do with innovation in constitutional interpretation after laboring for years in the shadow of the United States Supreme Court.

A significant portion of all of the courts' dockets was made up of criminal cases. The Arizona Supreme Court was primarily a court of criminal appeals. Exactly half of all the issues raised on the Arizona court concerned state statutes on criminal law and procedure. When issues concerning federal and state constitutional protection are added to the statutory issues, almost 75 percent of the work of the Arizona court was devoted to criminal justice. The New Jersey Supreme Court was least likely to hear criminal appeals: only 16.1 percent of its docket was made up of appeals of criminal procedure. Judicial activism scores on criminal cases were uniformly low. An unusual feature of the criminal cases is the fact that the New Jersey court outranks the California court in activism in this area of the law. The evaluation of the courts on the various measures of performance in criminal cases appears in Table A.8 (see appendix).

The low level of activism in criminal cases is explained by the presence of a constitutional claim in many of the cases. A reading of the cases showed that criminal defendants have a tendency to raise three general kinds of issues on appeal and that most cases showed a similar pattern of challenges. Generally, a criminal defendant will first allege a violation of state or federal constitutional rights in a pre-trial procedure. For example, a claim will be made that evidence was obtained without a warrant or probable cause, or that a confession was involuntary due to defects in *Miranda* warnings. If the supreme court rejected these arguments—and it usually did—the defendant next claimed some procedural defects at trial. A popular claim of this type is the allegation that the judge failed to give the appropriate or the standardized jury instructions. The supreme courts usually looked with disfavor on these arguments as well. When all else had failed—and it usually did—the defendant would argue that the sentence imposed by the trial court was excessive in light of statutory limitations or the defendant's past record or character. This final type of argument was almost universally rejected by the state courts of last resort. With the occasional exception of some New Jersey and California decisions, the bulk of the decisions of the state courts could scarcely be called "pro-criminal defendant." Since the crime control philosophy of recent Burger Court decisions was found suitable to the resolution of these cases, the state justices rarely invoked state constitutional provisions. The infrequent use of independent and adequate state grounds accounts for the low judicial activism scores seen in Table A.8.

For most of the six state supreme courts, the lowest levels of judicial activism were found in criminal constitutional cases, as seen in Table A.9 (see appendix). Here, criminal constitutional cases are those which presented an issue concerning the Fourth, Fifth, Sixth or Eighth Amendments to the federal Constitution or their state constitutional counterparts, or any other state constitutional guarantees of the rights of criminal defendants. The table reveals the overall reluctance of the state supreme courts to invoke purely state-derived protections for criminal defendants. The California Supreme Court, which has achieved some notoriety as a protector of civil rights and liberties, used independent and adequate state grounds in only 20.0 percent of its decisions.[6] The Michigan and New Jersey courts invoked independent and adequate state grounds only 14.3 percent and 8.3 percent of the time, respectively. The usually less activist courts did particularly poorly in these cases. For example, not a single criminal constitutional case decided by the Kentucky Court of Appeals rested on purely state grounds. I suspect that Arizona's and Nebraska's percentage scores on the use of independent and adequate state grounds do not reflect efforts to enhance the protection of federal rights as envisioned by Justice Brennan. Both state constitutions include provisions with no precise federal counterpart. For example, the Arizona constitution prohibits judicial commentary on trial proceedings to the jury. I believe that the few instances of the use of independent and adequate state grounds in Arizona and Nebraska do not represent the creation of new state standards for federally guaranteed civil rights. Instead, these decisions represent the interpretation of state constitutional provisions with no federal counterpart, usually to the dissatisfaction of the criminal defendant. The overall judicial activism scores for the states also are indicative of the poor performance of the state courts in criminal constitutional cases. Only the score of the New Jersey court equalled or surpassed its scores on other issue areas. However, this phenomenon is the result of the New Jersey court's tendency to include numerous citations of other state precedents or the scholarly literature in its opinions rather than the frequent use of independent and adequate state grounds.

An examination of the criminal constitutional cases also reveals some interesting patterns concerning dissent and reversal rates. The states scoring highest on judicial activism—New Jersey, Michigan and California—have the greatest likelihood of reversing the decisions of the lower courts. The relatively high reversal rate of these courts may be taken as an indication of civil libertarianism as defined in terms of pro-criminal defendant decisions according to the following argument. In the vast majority of criminal cases, the origin of an appeal was the conviction of the defendant. As discussed earlier in this chapter, the defendant will argue for the presence of a number of constitutional and procedural errors in the trial to the appellate court. Thomas J. Davies (1982), in a study of California intermediate appellate courts, has shown that there seems to exist among intermediate appellate court justices a norm of affirmance of trial court decision. This norm is apparently a product of a number of factors: the general assumption of guilt in the criminal justice system, the harmless error rule, large caseloads and commitment to *stare decisis*. If Davies is correct, then we may assume that the majority of intermediate appellate court decisions represent affirmation of the defendant's convictions. Therefore, high reversal rates of intermediate appellate court decisions in criminal cases may be associated with the supreme court's tendency to agree with the criminal defendant as to the presence of procedural and constitutional defects at trial. If this argument is correct, it is possible that the California, Michigan and New Jersey courts were using the federal Constitution, even in this day of the conservative Burger Court, to protect the rights of criminal defendants. Therefore, the low frequency of the use of independent and adequate state grounds should not be taken as an absolute indicator of the reluctance of these courts to serve civil libertarian causes. It must be remembered, however, that the choice to ground a decision in federal law opens the door to review by the United States Supreme Court, which may overturn liberal interpretations of federal constitutional guarantees. The Arizona Supreme Court presents a different case in its relation to lower courts. The Arizona court overturned the decisions of the lower court a mere 18.2 percent of the time. The low incidence of independent and adequate state grounds, combined with low reversal rates, may be taken as indicators of the conservative, crime control posture of the Arizona court.

In 1975, neither the Kentucky nor the Nebraska judicial system included an intermediate appellate court. Furthermore, the Nebraska Supreme Court possessed virtually no discretion in choosing criminal cases for review. It may be suggested, then, that at least for the Nebraska court, and to a little lesser extent for the Kentucky Court of Appeals, these courts were providing the same review function in criminal cases as the intermediate appellate courts of the other four states. The low reversal rates for the Nebraska and Kentucky courts are understandable in terms of Davies' norm of the affirmation of trial court decisions.

The California, Michigan and New Jersey courts showed unusual levels of disagreement among the justices in criminal constitutional cases, as indicated by the fractions of unanimous opinions rendered by the courts. While almost 43 percent of all such cases were decided unanimously in California, only one-quarter of such cases were similarly decided in New Jersey and a mere 14.3 percent in the usually divided Michigan court. I believe the particularly high levels of dissent in criminal cases is caused by the controversial nature of most criminal justice cases. Courts of last resort with discretion in the choice of cases for review and an intermediate appellate screening of cases can select the most problematic cases for consideration. Since problematic cases probably engender more disagreement among the justices than routine cases, high levels of dissent and non-unanimous decisions can be expected. If high reversal rates of the intermediate appellate court's decisions are indicative of pro-criminal defendant decisions of the supreme court, then there is an additional source of disagreement among the justices. The New Jersey, California and Michigan courts may have been rendering liberal decisions in a climate of conservativism encouraged by the United States Supreme Court and endorsed by a large proportion of the American public. Therefore, criminal constitutional cases may create additional conflicts in judicial values, which extend to such matters as the appropriate relationship between the state and federal Court and the extent to which justices in a democracy should heed public opinion. In other words, these three supreme courts were considering hard cases in which the requirements of the law are uncertain and which presented additional opportunities for conflict over judicial values.

The six supreme courts decided a total of 304 constitutional cases in 1975. A case is considered to be constitutional if a federal or state constitutional claim is present among the three issues coded for each case. Despite the popular association of supreme courts with constitutional interpretation, less than one-third (30.4 percent) of all cases embodied a constitutional claim. What is even more noteworthy is the large fraction of constitutional cases that concerned criminal justice. More than 41 percent of all the constitutional cases were devoted to procedural guarantees for criminal defendants. The work of the Arizona Supreme Court seldom extended beyond the interpretation of the Fourth and Fifth Amendments to the federal Constitution. As will be seen in some detail in Chapter 5, all six state supreme courts rarely, if ever, dealt with the First Amendment or equal protection issues.[7] It probably is safe to assume that adjudication of these issues remained the purview of federal courts in 1975. Again, patterns of judicial activism, reversal rates and levels of intracourt disagreement remained the same for constitutional cases as in the other issue areas. The most activist courts—New Jersey, California and Michigan—were also most likely to reverse the decisions of lower courts and to show disagreement among the justices. The Nebraska Supreme Court showed an unusually high dissent rate (dissents filed in 21.9 percent of cases) in constitutional cases, but virtually all of these dissents were penned by maverick justice Hale McCown. On the whole, the state courts rarely invoked independent and adequate state grounds, and the relatively high activism scores of the California and New Jersey courts were more the products of the use of sister state precedents and law review articles rather than the reliance on state constitutional law. However, low judicial activism scores should not be construed to rule out creativity with federal constitutional provisions. Unfortunately, this data set does not allow for a comparison of federal and state holdings on the same federal constitutional provisions. The comparison of the performance of the six state courts in all constitutional cases is presented in Table A.10 (see Appendix).

There are virtually no statistically significant differences among the courts if only non-criminal constitutional cases are considered. Reversal rates, fractions of cases containing concurring opinions, the use of independent and adequate state grounds and judicial activism scores are approximately the same for all six states. The only real difference among the courts arose from levels of dissent, and here the differences follow the pattern seen in other issue areas. Once again, the Michigan Supreme Court was the most badly divided court, while again the Arizona and Kentucky courts showed the greatest tendency toward unanimity among the justices.

The similarity among the courts may be explained in terms of the nature of the non-criminal constitutional cases. Generally, these cases involved challenges to state legislation, usually some form of economic regulation, under various provisions of the federal and state constitutions. In each state, the justices attached the traditional high presumption of validity to such actions, and, accordingly, they were reluctant to declare a regulation unconstitutional. This norm of judicial deference to the legislature probably accounts for the similar performance of the courts. Of course, there were some instances in which the courts did impose stricter standards of scrutiny, but challenges to legislation involving fundamental rights or "suspect categories" were quite rare. Moreover, the imposition of the higher standard of review did not necessarily foreordain a declaration of unconstitutionality. Some of these cases will be explored in the next chapter.

In this chapter, I have compared the performance of six state supreme courts and suggested some explanations for the sources of variation. Here, I have used three different measures of state court performance: reversal rates of lower court decisions, levels of intracourt disagreement and judicial activism scores. I believe that some of the differences among the courts may be accounted for by some of the variables contained in the model presented in Chapter 1. Contextual variables, such as political culture, the state's socioeconomic diversity, internal unity and party competition, may account for the levels of dissent and reversals. Elements of this theory are supported by the work of Jaros and Canon (1971). Institutional variables, particularly the presence or absence of an intermediate appellate court, also may influence dissents and reversal rates. The importance of intermediate appellate courts in the state judiciary has been noted by Davies (1982), Kagan et al. (1978) and Atkins and Glick (1976). Generally, intermediate appellate courts should be associated with increased dissents and reversals by the state court of last resort. The findings contained in this chapter lend support to this theory. Finally, the personal characteristics and interactions among the justices also may help to explain dissent rates. Jaros and Canon (1971) have shown that social background characteristics of state supreme court justices have an impact on dissent rates. I have suggested some additional factors to be considered in examining dissent. First, maverick justices may account for a disproportionate number of dissents and concurrences. Maverick justices feel compelled to produce extra opinion even when these opinions seem to add little to the exposition of the law. I can only assume that this behavior is a function of the personality of the justices. Also, the presence of a maverick justice on a court will be a random occurrence. Second, state supreme courts may operate under different decision-making norms. Fenno's (1973) work on congressional committees may provide some guidance in the development of theory of decision-making norms on state supreme courts.

I have done little in the chapter to explain variations in judicial activism. The next chapter examines the work of the six courts in some detail and suggest some reasons for variations in judicial activism.

NOTES

1. See, for example, Atkins, Burton M., and Henry R. Glick. 1976. Environmental and Structural Variables as Determinants of Issues in State Courts

of Last Resort. *American Political Science Review*, 20:97–115; and Kagan, Robert A., et al. 1978. The Evolution of State Supreme Courts. *Michigan Law Review*, 76:961–1001.

2. The Kagan et al. classification system is as follows: (1) property, contract, collection or corporate law; (2) criminal or public law; (3) private torts, except workmen's compensation; (4) constitutional cases. The Atkins and Glick system contains the following categories: (1) criminal; (2) civil liberty; (3) economic regulation; (4) private economic; (5) private non-economic.

3. Under Elazar's system, the higher the numerical score, the lower the internal unity of the state. The scores of the states under consideration here are: Arizona (6), California (8), Kentucky (7), Michigan (11), Nebraska (7) and New Jersey (8).

4. For a description of the mechanics of judicial decision-making and the desirability of unanimous decisions see: Murphy, Walter F. 1964. *Elements of Judicial Strategy*. Chicago: University of Chicago Press. A case study of the importance of unanimity in a landmark decision in which the United States Supreme Court faced the prospect of massive resistance to its decision may be found in: Kluger, Richard. 1975. *Simple Justice: The History of Brown v. Board of Education and Black America's Struggle for Equality*. New York: Vintage Books.

5. The reader is referred to the appropriate pie-charts in Chapter 5 for the source of these percentage comparisons.

6. I am assuming that the use of independent and adequate state grounds is representative of greater constitutional protection for civil rights and liberties. This assumption is based on the recognition that the Supremacy Clause of the federal Constitution prohibits state creation of standards less than the minimal requirements of the federal Bill of Rights. Consequently, the use of independent and adequate state grounds implies, at the very least, equality with federal constitutional guarantees.

7. The precise breakdown of issues for all the courts according to the detailed coding scheme is available from the author upon request.

5. A Closer Look at Six Courts

This chapter gives the reader a closer look at the work of six state supreme courts. I examine the decisions of the courts in light of the factors related to supreme court performance outlined in the model proposed in Chapter 1. I suggest that state internal unity, political culture and institutional characteristics of the state judiciary are related to the performance of the courts although the relationships are far from perfect.

A few words of caution are in order for this chapter. The arguments here cannot be "proven" or "disproven" by anything in the data set. The chapter is primarily an impressionistic application of the model of performance. The purpose here is to demonstrate the uses and limits of the model and to offer a subjective evaluation of the performance of the courts in light of the model. No claim is made that the arguments can apply to all courts at all times or that certain cultural or institutional characteristics will necessarily cause certain variations in court performance. However, the chapter enables the reader to develop a qualitative appreciation of the differences in performance and a sense of some of the possible sources of that variation. The reader should take some comfort in the knowledge that these impressions are derived from the reading and coding of more than 1,200 full opinions, rather than personal whimsy. Conclusions on the performance of the courts and recommendations for the improvement of state courts of last resort are reserved for the final chapter.[1]

ARIZONA: A CLASS I STATE

Elazar (1966) has developed a twelve-point scale to rate the degree of internal unity of a state: the lower the score, the higher the degree of internal unity and, theoretically, the greater the ability of the state to resist federal encroachment. Arizona scores six on this scale, which, according to Elazar, indicates that the state is unified but tends to follow national patterns. The use of water resources in this desert state should be the major concern and source of internal unity. However, if there is one dominant issue for the Arizona Supreme Court, it is the control of smuggling, both narcotics and "illegal immigrants," from Mexico. Figure 5.1 reveals the large fraction of state criminal procedural issues addressed by the Arizona court. Although these issues run the gamut from arrest to judicial discretion in sentencing, the bulk of the convictions involves narcotics. Of all the federal constitutional issues raised, 24.7 percent concerned the Fourth Amendment's requirement of probable cause and prohibition against unreasonable searches and seizures; 91.3 percent involved the rights of criminal defendants. Even the tiny fraction of federal statutory cases touched on the problem of illegal drugs and the power of federal Fish and Wildlife agents to turn drug offenders in national parks over to state authorities (*State v. Goldberg*, 112 Ariz. 202, 540 P.2d 674). Contrary to Elazar's expectations, only a single case, *Neal v. Hunt*, 112 Ariz. 307, 541 P.2d 559, concerned the allocation of water resources. Arizona does seem to follow national conservative judicial trends: the state scores lowest overall in judicial activism and lowest in activism in criminal cases.

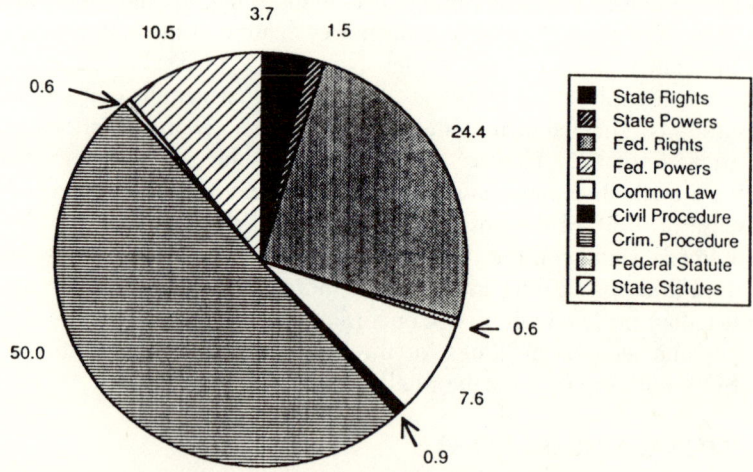

Figure 5.1 Issues in Arizona Supreme Court, 1975

In constitutional cases, the justices of the Arizona court invoked independent and adequate state grounds 9.2 percent of the time. Undoubtedly, the crime control rulings of the Burger Court fit the needs of a state beset with smuggling problems. Consequently, there is no incentive for the justices to develop and rely on innovative interpretations of state criminal constitutional law.

Arizona is an amalgamation of the Traditionalistic and Moralistic political cultures although the culture is dominated by the Traditionalistic aspect. There are two institutional features of the Arizona court system which square with expectations for a Moralistic culture: judicial recruitment at the supreme court level by gubernatorial appointment from merit lists and a judicial qualifications commission to supervise the lower courts. There are also a large number of criminal cases, which is also consistent with the expectations for "M" culture. However, there is no detectable evidence of Traditionalistic features in Arizona. In fact, the court system of Arizona approximates the American Bar Association model of a modern court system: there are two courts of limited jurisdiction, an intermediate appellate court and a single court of last resort. Arizona scores nine on the judicial professionalism scale, which is above the national average and more consistent with the expectations for an Individualistic, rather than Traditionalistic, culture.

My qualitative and quantitative assessment of the Arizona Supreme Court is that it is not a very activist or creative state court. It consistently scores low on the judicial activism scale, and it relies almost entirely on the Supreme Court for guidance in constitutional cases. The one instance of judicial review in Arizona, *Thorton v. Carson*, 111 Ariz. 490, 533 P.2d 657, struck down the state's replevin statute on purely federal Fourteenth Amendment due process grounds.[2] When looking for information from other states and legal scholars, the justices generally went no further than their neighbor, California, or their own state university law review. I would suggest three possible institutional explanations for this situation: the Arizona Supreme Court was underpaid, understaffed and overworked. The justices were compensated $37,000 for their services, which is $900 below the national average. This is scarcely an incentive for creative research. There were two law clerks authorized for each justice, but only seven secretaries, librarians and other clerical workers to assist the court, a situation which does not make difficult legal research any easier. Finally, the entire docket of the supreme court, en banc and in panel, was 212 cases. This figure is nearly 25 percent higher than the number of cases handled by the California Supreme Court or the Kentucky Court of Appeals. The full court considered 170 cases while the remainder was argued before three-justice panels. These panel cases were usually routine contract and private tort cases which were decided in all instances without dissent. This practice seems terribly wasteful of supreme court resources, especially since Arizona has an intermediate appellate court which should resolve such minor cases. The work of the Arizona Supreme Court sitting in division is summarized in Figure 5.2.

CALIFORNIA: A CLASS V STATE

California scores nine on Elazar's internal unity scale; therefore, it should be less capable than highly unified states such as Arizona, Kentucky and Nebraska of resisting federal encroachment on state politics and policies. Yet, here are found some of the highest levels of state judicial activism as seen in Chapter 4. California was the most willing of the six states to evoke explicitly its own constitution to impose stricter standards for the protection of individual rights and liberties than required by the federal Constitution, as interpreted by the Burger Court. The California court was particularly willing to invoke Article I, sec-

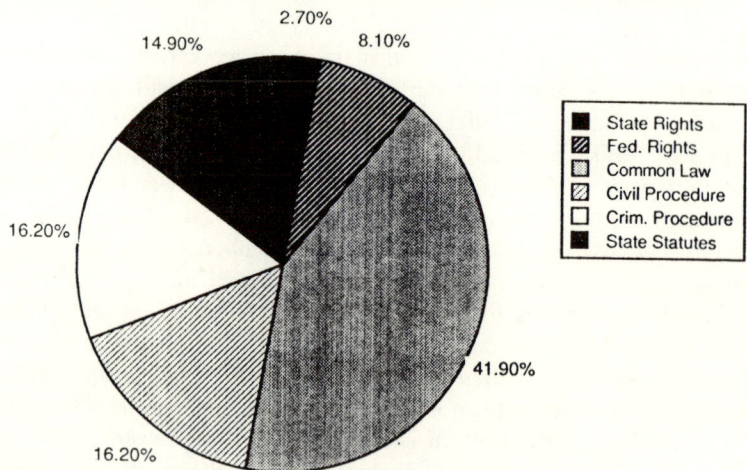

Figure 5.2 Issues in Arizona Supreme Court, 1975 (Panel Cases Only)

tion 13 of the California Constitution to avoid the narrow interpretation of the federal Fourth Amendment by the Burger Court. For example, in *People v. Brisedine*, 12 Ca.3d. 528, 119 Cal. Rptr. 315, 531 P.2d 1099, the California court used the California constitution to limit the scope of permissible warrantless searches for weapons and contraband. The majority, speaking through Justice Mosk, recognized the federal standard for "pat down" searches developed in *Terry v. Ohio*, 392 U.S. 1, 88 S.Ct. 1868, 20 L.Ed.2d 889 (1968) but indicated the California constitution requires a "more exacting standard." Justice Mosk was careful to assert that such an approach to the problem of warrantless searches was justified, and perhaps even compelled, by a new provision of the California constitution, Article I, section 24, enacted in November, 1965, which declares that California rights and liberties are not dependent on federal rights and liberties. In later cases, the court reiterated its approach to searches and seizures by restricting warrantless searches of automobiles and their drivers.[3] The California court also refused to reach federal constitutional claims in reviewing criminal sentences in light of prohibitions in both the federal and state constitutions against cruel and unusual punishment. In *People v. Wingo*, 14 Ca.3d 169, 121 Cal. Rptr. 97, 534 P.2d 100, and *In re Rodriguez*, 14 Ca.3d 639, 122 Cal. Rptr. 552, 537 P.2d 384, the California court indicated its willingness to evaluate the length of time served by a prisoner under an indeterminate sentence under a proportionality principle which the court believed is required by Article I, section 17 of the California constitution.

While internal unity may not be useful in explaining the California court's relationship with the United States Supreme Court, the concept may be useful in explaining the diversity of the court's docket, as seen in Figure 5.3. Unlike Arizona, where the problems arising from smuggling operations seemed to have been the major concern of the state judiciary, California was faced with no single overriding issue for resolution. Elazar has suggested that the allocation of water resources should be the major source of whatever internal unity exists in California. However, the California court considered but a single water resources case in 1975: *City of Los Angeles v. City of San Fernando*, 14 Ca.3d 199, 123 Cal. Rptr. 1, 637 P.2d 1975.

California is a Moralistic-Individualistic political culture with the emphasis on Moralistic. There are Moralistic elements to the institutions of the California judicial system: a merit element in appellate

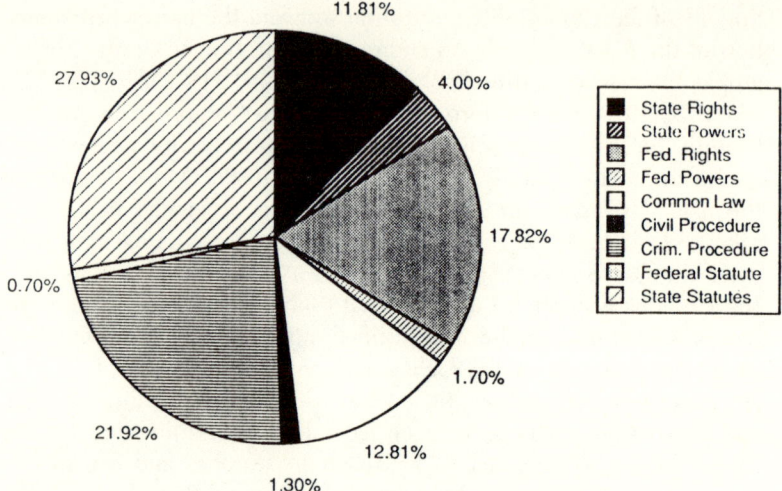

Figure 5.3 Issues in California Supreme Court, 1975

court recruitment, nonpartisan elections for trial court judges, and a judicial qualifications commission for the regulation of the lower judiciary. There are Individualistic elements as well. The justices of the California Supreme Court were paid $57,985 plus a built-in cost of living adjustment. The court system scores a nine on the professionalism scale. There were a total of fifty-five law clerks, secretaries and librarians to assist the justices in 1975. Political culture also may be reflected in the nature of the cases handled by the California court. A large fraction of the state statutory cases concern the regulation of the bar, and in these decisions the court showed little tolerance for attorney corruption. In fact, 32.9 percent of all non-procedural statutory cases involved attorney discipline, as compared with 0.06 in Kentucky. However, the Moralistic element is not present in criminal cases, as illustrated by the *Brisedine* decision and its progeny. This due-process rather than crime-control emphasis may be a reflection of the Individualistic element on California political culture, which exalts the right of the individual over the ideal of the community. California has the highest percentage of First Amendment and equal protection cases of the six courts, although overall the percentage of these cases was quite small. In California, 4.8 percent of the cases contained a federal equal protection element, and, in the area of First Amendment

A Closer Look at Six Courts

freedoms, 3.0 percent of the cases embodied a federal constitutional claim and 2.4 percent a state constitutional claim. These small numbers problems may represent the traditional reliance on the federal Court for such civil libertarian claims. Also consistent with the expectation for an Individualistic culture, California showed a high rate of challenges to administrative regulation and procedures: 14.6 percent of all state statutory cases touched on administrative law.

The opinions of the California Supreme Court were characterized by relatively high levels of activism, disagreement and craftsmanship. In every kind of case, California scores highest on judicial activism. The California court also exercised judicial review more than any other state in this study. Three cases—*People v. Burnick*, 14 Ca.3d 306, 121 Cal. Rptr. 488, 535 P.2d 352; *People v. Feagley*, 14 Ca.3d 338, 121 Cal. Rptr. 509, 535 P.2d 373; *People v. Bonneville*, 14 Ca.3d 384, 121 Cal. Rptr. 540, 535 P.2d 404—declared various portions of the state's Mentally Disordered Sex Offender Statute unconstitutional under the Fourteenth Amendment's due process guarantee and a similar guarantee contained in Article I, section 7 of the California constitution. *Gould v. Gruble*, 14 Ca.3d 661, 122 Cal. Rptr. 377, 536 P.2d 1337 struck down a Santa Monica municipal election law requiring incumbents' names to be placed at the top of the ballot as a violation of federal and state equal protection requirements. In an unusual case, *Dupuy v. Superior Court*, 15 Ca.3d 410, 124 Cal. Rptr. 900, 541 P.2d 540, the court actually nullified Article XIII, section 15 of the California constitution which prohibited the issuing of injunction to prevent the collection of taxes, arguing that the state constitution must yield to federal requirements of due process. Even cases involving the common law revealed creativity, painstaking legal research and judicial craftsmanship. *Li v. Yellow Cab Co.*, 13 Ca.3d 804, 119 Cal. Rptr. 377, 536 P.2d 1337, a decision which abolished the "all or nothing" rule of contributory negligence, surveyed seven different law reviews, the law of negligence in nine states, English common law and the Code Napoleon. The single water rights case, *City of Los Angeles v. City of San Fernando*, cited earlier, considered the California constitution's provision on water rights, the state water code statute, English common law and Spanish and Mexican law on pueblo rights.

There are a number of institutional features of the California judicial system which probably contribute to the high quality of court performance. The high salaries and long term of office (twelve years) not only make the position of supreme court justice attractive to talented legal professionals, but also provide the incentive to study and grow within the career. The twelve-year term also provides a shield from popular and political pressures, although the state recall provision detracts somewhat from complete judicial independence. Finally, the large support staff provided to the justices greatly enhances the research capability of the court and, consequently, the craftsmanship of the opinions.

KENTUCKY: A CLASS III STATE

Kentucky's political culture is a combination of the dominant cultures of Arizona and New Jersey—Traditionalistic and Individualistic, with the accent on tradition. Kentucky scores seven on Elazar's internal unity scale, placing it between the unified Arizona and the diverse Michigan. Elazar sees the maintenance of Kentucky's established political patterns as the major source of the state's internal unity, and there is some evidence to support this view as applied to the state judiciary. Prior to a major reform effort in 1975, which eventually brought about a major constitutional revision of the court system, there was strong county level control of the courts, and judicial positions were authorized for political reasons rather than need. There was a baroque system of limited jurisdiction courts—police courts, peace courts, county courts, quarterly courts, justice-of-the-peace courts and fiscal courts—charged with county governance. There was also no intermediate court of appeals. The 1975 changes were designed to bring the structure of the Kentucky court system into line with the American Bar Association's model. Court reformers in Kentucky found through public opinion polls that citizens were enthusiastic about the prospect of making their judicial system more efficient and economical (consistent with Individualistic cultural values) but feared the implementation of centralized administration and the loss of control (consistent with Traditionalistic values). Eventually, judicial reform was achieved through support from the two gubernatorial candidates and voters in metropolitan districts, despite strong resistance from residents of the hill country who have a "tradition of embracing the Anglo-Saxon magisterial system of justice."[4] If there was a dominant issue that unites Kentucky present in the docket of the Court of Appeals, it is land use

A Closer Look at Six Courts

and its consequences. Of the non-procedural state statutory cases shown in Figure 5.4, 13.8 percent involved zoning or property disputes and 26.6 percent workmen's compensation cases, all but three of which arose from coal miners' claims of black lung disease.

The institutional features of the pre-reform Kentucky system reflected both the Traditionalistic and Individualistic facets of the state's political culture. The "T" element was apparent in the antiquated system of courts, reinforced by a strong heritage of local control. Even justices of the court of appeals were elected by judicial district. The state also scored seven on the professionalism scale, a point below the national average. The "I" culture was seen in the lack of a merit system and any kind of commission on judicial qualifications. The Court of Appeals was well staffed; there were thirty-five law clerks, secretaries and librarians authorized in 1975 but underpaid. Justices earned $31,500 in 1975, compared with the national average of more than $37,000.

Figure 5.4 shows the extent to which the Kentucky Court of Appeals was not a constitutional court. A mere 14 percent of the issues considered were constitutional, and the bulk of these cases involved the federal, rather than the state, Constitution. Essentially, the work of the court was statutory interpretation and the development of the common law. These factors account for the high fraction of cases in-

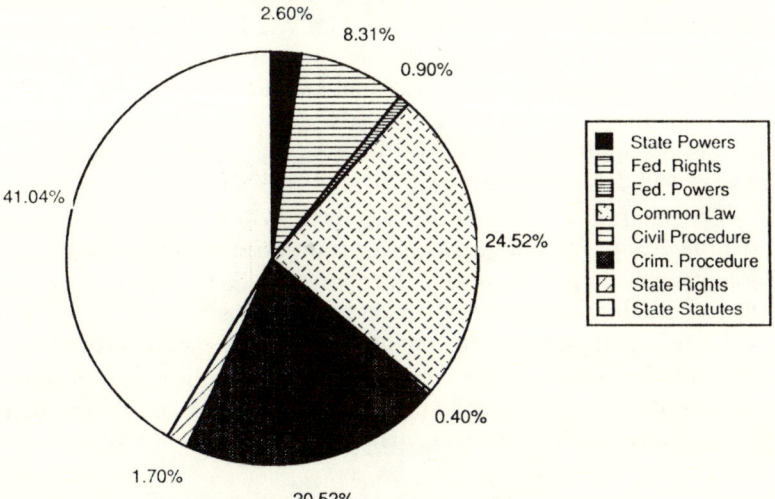

Figure 5.4 Issues in Kentucky Court of Appeals, 1975

volving independent and adequate state grounds seen in the analysis in Chapter 4.

A qualitative assessment of the opinion of the court shows the wide variety in the kinds of cases and the craftsmanship of opinions. Some trivial cases bordered on the ridiculous. In one instance—*Parham v. Commonwealth*, 520 S.W.2d 327—the justices evaluated snapshots of a 1964 Ford to determine whether it was worth more than $25. The court declared that the automobile "was not a junker," that the justices were no more ignorant of the value of used cars than the average layperson and, therefore, the defendant was guilty of felony arson under the statutory definition of the crime. However, the court did exhibit some creativity in the area of judge-made law. Kentucky had no statute governing the admission of expert testimony in medical malpractice suits, so the Court of Appeals adopted the federal rules of evidence in civil procedure to govern Kentucky trials.[5] There were two constitutional cases of interest decided by the court. The first—*Stephens v. Commonwealth*, 522 S.W.2d 181—reinforced the traditional administration of justice in Kentucky. The court allowed the admission of incriminating evidence which was the fruit of a search conducted pursuant to a defective warrant issued by a non-lawyer magistrate, ignorant of the requirements of the Fourth Amendment. The other case—*Department of Natural Resources and Environmental Protection v. No. 8 Limited of Virginia*, 528 S.W.2d 684—declared Chapter 350 of the Kentucky Revised Statutes unconstitutional. This statute, which regulated strip mining, was found not to be a legitimate exercise of the police power but, instead, a taking of private property in violation of the Fifth Amendment of the federal Constitution and Articles 13, 19 and 242 of the Kentucky constitution.

The major problems with the Kentucky Court of Appeals probably stemmed from the antiquated lower court system and the lack of an intermediate court of appeals. The court considered a few more cases than the California court and substantially less than the Arizona court, but it is hard to imagine the amount of time and energy spent screening cases for review and overseeing a large, complicated, and sometimes untrained, judiciary. The constitutional overhaul of the Kentucky courts in 1975, however, may dramatically alter the performance of the court of appeals.

MICHIGAN: A CLASS VI STATE

Of all the states under consideration, Michigan scores the lowest in internal unity. In fact, Michigan, New York and Illinois score the lowest in internal unity in the United States. Consequently, Michigan should be least capable of fending off federal encroachment on state politics, but the Michigan Supreme Court ranked with California and New Jersey on the judicial activism scale. The lack of internal unity in the state of Michigan may, however, be a factor in the explanation of the proclivity of the supreme court justices to dissent so frequently along party lines. Elazar believes that whatever internal unity does exist in Michigan is a general consensus on the importance of economic development. There was some evidence of the importance of economic issues in the Michigan court in 1975. More than 30 percent of the court's docket was concerned with state regulatory statutes, and 24.1 percent of all regulatory cases embodied labor-related issues such as workmen's compensation, unemployment and retirement. Needless to say, the court was usually badly divided over the proper resolution of these cases, with Democratic justices taking the party's traditional pro-labor stance and the Republican justices aligning themselves with business interests.

Elazar describes the political culture as Moralistic. According to the model developed in Chapter 1, a number of institutional characteristics of the state judiciary should be associated with a Moralistic political culture: judicial selection by merit system or nonpartisan election, supervision of the courts by qualifications commissions and comparatively low salaries. The Michigan court system features two of these theoretical characteristics. Judges and justices are chosen by nonpartisan election, although it must be noted that these judicial elections are nonpartisan in name only since the parties openly nominate and endorse candidates. The judiciary in Michigan is supervised by a judicial tenure commission which can make recommendations to the supreme court for the discipline or removal of judges. However, Michigan court justices earned $43,000 in 1975, a salary well above the national average and among the highest in the nation.

Given Elazar's description of a Moralistic political culture, it was hypothesized that a large number of challenges to the nature of government intervention in public and private affairs would appear in the dockets of courts of Moralistic cultures. Numerous criminal cases also should be considered by the courts and few of these cases resolved in favor of the criminal defendant. The largest fraction of the decisions of the Michigan Supreme Court involved state regulatory statutes, but only 17.2 percent of the docket concerned criminal procedure (see Figure 5.5). Moreover, only six of the federal constitutional issues (26.0 percent) concerned the criminal procedural guarantees of the Fourth, Fifth and Sixth Amendments, and only two state constitutional issues (10.0 percent) concerned stated counterparts to the Fourth and Sixth Amendments. These findings on the small percentages of criminal cases in the Michigan court are not consistent with the expectations for a moralistic political culture. Finally, the Michigan judicial system scores a five on the judicial professionalism scale. This score is well below the national average of eight but consistent with the expectations for a Moralistic political culture with its ideal of the amateur citizen-politician.

A qualitative assessment of the opinions of the Michigan court revealed opinions which were generally well crafted but often characterized by sharp language directed to any justices who happened to have disagreed with its author. The most notable and acidic dialogues took place between former governor and Democratic Justice Williams and Republican Justice Coleman. The justices all drew from a wide range

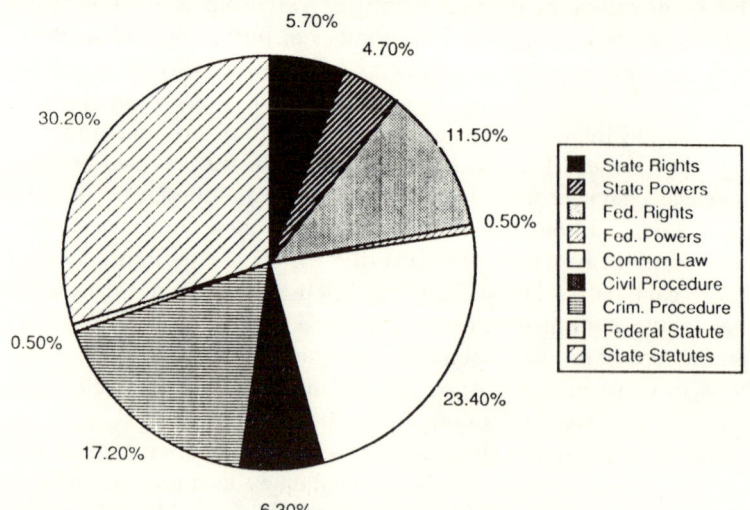

Figure 5.5 Issues in Michigan Supreme Court, 1975

A Closer Look at Six Courts

of legal periodicals and sister state precedents, especially California, Illinois and New York, in writing their opinions. It is interesting to note that that Michigan court looked frequently to Illinois and New York, the other states lowest in internal unity, for guidance.

Michigan is the only state court of the six to grant advisory opinions. However, it is save to say that the justices were extremely reluctant to grant advice to the legislature or governor. The court construed the constitutional requirements for an opinion very strictly in order to avoid, whenever possible, granting advisory opinions. If the request for the opinion did not present a specific question or was not made after the enactment of a statute but before its effective date, as specified in Article III, section 8 of the 1963 Michigan constitution, the court declined to grant the advisory opinion.[6] When the court chose to grant its advice, its guidance was of limited utility. In *Advisory Opinion re Constitutionality of 1974 P.A. 242*, 394 Mich. 41, 228 N.W.2d 772, only four justices could agree on an opinion on the constitutionality of state aid, in the form of textbooks and supplies, to non-public schools under the federal First Amendment or its state analog, Article VIII, section 2 of the Michigan constitution.

The most interesting decisions of the Michigan Supreme Court were the few examples of judicial review. In *Manistee Bank and Trust Co. v. McGowan*, 394 Mich. 655, 232 N.W.2d 636, the court declared Michigan's Automobile Guest Passenger Statute, which had been enacted in 1929, a violation of the equal protection requirements of Article I, section 2 of the state constitution. The companion case, *Longnecker v. Noordyk-Mooney, Inc.*, 394 Mich. 696, 232 N.W.2d 654, extended the holding in *Manistee Bank* to the Aviation Guest Passenger Statute. The Michigan Supreme Court also struck down, under federal and state equal protection guarantees, a number of zoning ordinances which restricted trailers and trailer parks in certain municipalities.[7] The court also examined the constitutionality of administrative procedures for the revocation of drivers' licenses under federal and state due process requirements. In *Crampton v. Department of State*, 395 Mich. 347, 235 N.W.2d 352, the court ruled that "appeals board panels which are membered by full-time law enforcement officials are not fair and impartial tribunals to adjudge a law enforcement dispute between a citizen and a police officer." Finally, the court held that the legislature cannot constitutionally delegate authority to the Michigan Employees Relation Commission to order compulsory arbitration of police and firefighter labor disputes. The majority of justices agreed that such a delegation would allow an arbiter to make important political and policy choices in violation of the principle of separation of powers and the state constitutional "home rule" guarantee.[8]

If there is a problem with the Michigan Supreme Court, it lies in the divisive nature of state politics. The struggle between labor and business, between Democrats and Republicans gets translated into ideological disagreements on the supreme court. Michigan justices dissented and concurred more than any other court. The Michigan court also had more decisions decided by one vote than any other court. What this means is the law is never settled in Michigan: the replacement of one justice at the next "nonpartisan" election could swing case outcomes in the opposite direction. This potentially volatile situation can only detract from the prestige of the court and the authority with which it speaks.

NEBRASKA: A CLASS II STATE

Nebraska scores a seven on Elazar's internal unity scale, indicating a moderate ability to fend off federal encroachment on state policies. For Elazar, the rallying point in Nebraskan politics is general concern for agricultural problems. However, constitutional interpretation in Nebraska is almost completely governed by federal standards. As seen in Figure 5.6, only 3.1 percent of all issues raised before the Nebraska Supreme Court sitting en banc involved an interpretation of the state constitution. Only three issues considered state constitutional guarantee for the protection of individual rights and in these cases the supreme court held that the requirements of the Nebraska constitution are identical to the requirements in the federal Bill of Rights. The remaining instances of state constitutional interpretation dealt with legislative and judicial procedures and state economic policy. There was some indication of the state's concern with agricultural problems in a number of cases decided by the court. In a panel decision, the court refused to allow for civil remedies under the Fair Labor Standards Act for a fourteen-year-old boy injured in the course of farm work on a neighbor's farm.[9] A en banc decision limited recovery under an insurance policy when injuries resulted as part of a work exchange agreement during harvest time. The court declared this traditional exchange of labor between farm families "a neighborly and

A Closer Look at Six Courts   101

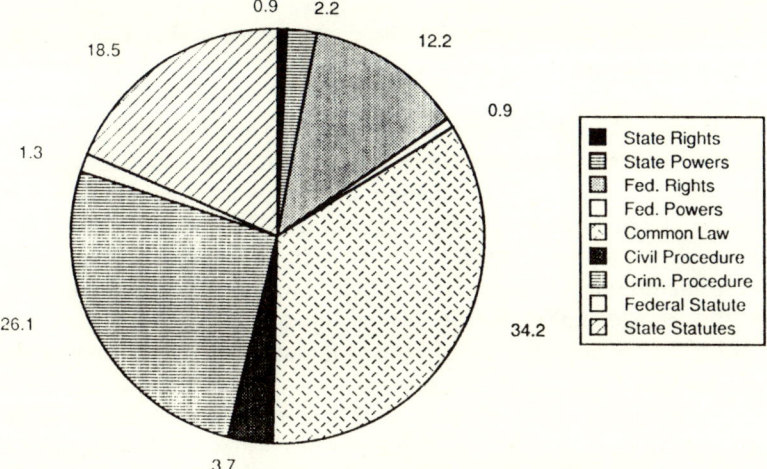

Figure 5.6 Issues in Nebraska Supreme Court, 1975

Christian thing to do" and, therefore, was unwilling to jeopardize these informal arrangements by opening the door to lawsuits over insurance coverage.[10]

The political culture of Nebraska is primarily Individualistic, but it includes some Moralistic overtones. However, the institutional features of the Nebraska state court system were more in line with expectations for a Moralistic political culture rather than the state's dominant Individualistic culture. In 1975, judges and justices were chosen by the Missouri Plan and were supervised by a judicial qualifications commission. The justices of the supreme court were paid $35,500, a figure slightly below the national average. The court system also scored seven on the judicial professionalism scale, a point below the national mean. There was also a large number of criminal cases decided by the supreme court, and these decisions revealed little sympathy for criminal defendants. Finally, there was little disagreement on the supreme court, and much of the dissent that did appear could be explained by the presence of a single justice. All of these characteristics of the Nebraska judiciary are consistent with the expectations for a Moralistic political culture. No evidence of Individualistic cultural values was apparent.

The entire docket of the Nebraska Supreme Court for 1975 was 362 cases. Of these cases, 280 were decided en banc and 82 in panel. The immense caseload was probably the consequence of the absence of an intermediate appellate court. The court did sit in panels made up of three supreme court justices and two district judges, but this arrangement seemed to do little to lessen the workload of an individual justice. Moreover, all district court decisions, as well as the decisions of juvenile and workmen's compensation courts, were appealable by right to the supreme court, en banc or in panel.[11] To compound the problems of the supreme court, the full court was required to review all non-unanimous decisions of the panels. This unusual situation is akin to the arrangement under the Federal Judiciary Act of 1789, in which United States Supreme Court justices found themselves reviewing decisions they had made riding circuit.

The opinions of the supreme court suffered under the weight of the number of cases that it was required to hear. Few legal periodicals or sister state precedents were cited by the court. A major problem for the court was the review of numerous criminal cases. Of all the federal constitutional issues raised in court, 81.7 percent concerned the rights of criminal defendants. A more problematic area for the court was the requirement that it review sentences imposed by trial court judges. Approximately 52.2 percent of all criminal cases involved sentence review, and, in all but a single case, the court found the defendant's contention "patently frivolous" or even "farcical." In one case, Justice Spencer complained about the role of inmate legal advisors in generating these hopeless cases which the court could not have avoided reviewing.[12]

There were a number of interesting cases decided by the supreme court in 1975. In *Nebraska Public Service Commission v. Chicago and N.W. Transportation Co.*, 193 Neb. 59, 225 N.W.2d 401, the court ruled that Title 49 of the Interstate Commerce Act preempted rules of the public service commission governing the distribution of railroad cars within the state. The court addressed the problem of the balance between free press and fair trial in *State v. Simants*, 194 Neb. 783, 236 N.W.2d 794, and attempted to issue guidelines governing the media covering a sensational multiple murder trial. It was in *Simants* that the court indicated:

The constitutional guarantees of freedom of speech and of the press and of the right to trial by an impartial jury are, in our judgment, the same under both the constitutions of this state and of the United States, and there is no need to differentiate between the two constitutions in this discussion.[13]

A Closer Look at Six Courts 103

The court also held that a motor vehicle statute which allowed police officers to stop automobiles randomly for license and registration inspection did not violate the requirements of the Fourth Amendment.[14] The Nebraska Supreme Court also considered a few equal protection cases. In *Richards v. Omaha Public Schools*, 194 Neb. 463, 232 N.W.2d 29, the court held that the refusal of the school board to treat pregnancy leave like any other sick leave did not amount to unconstitutional gender-based discrimination. The Nebraska court, just like the Michigan Supreme Court, deliberated equal protection challenges to the state's Motor Vehicle Guest Passenger Statutes, only with very different results. Unlike the Michigan court, the Nebraska justices found the statutes constitutional after carefully polling other jurisdictions and noting how other states were divided over the appropriate resolution of this issue.[15] Finally, the court showed some creativity with the common law. *Royal Indemnity Co. v. Aetna Casualty and Surety Co.*, 193 Neb. 752, 232 N.W.2d 29, put an end to a long-standing principle that there be no contribution between negligent joint tortfeasors. However, interesting cases, such as those just noted, constituted only a tiny fraction of the large caseload of the Nebraska Supreme Court.

The panel decisions of the court ranged from the usual disputes over contracts, negligence, divorce and wills, to several rather important cases concerning economic regulation (see Figure 5.7). For example, in one decision, the panel construed the Nebraska Budget Act to allow for taxpayers' suits but not to allow the recovery of attorney fees should the taxpayers' challenge to a budget enactment prove successful.[16] A panel also considered a novel case which involved the legality of supermarkets' participation, without authorization from the Public Service Commission, in an electronic money transfer service via computer terminals with local banks.[17] Another panel decision evaluated the relationship between regulations promulgated by the Public Service Commission and the standards required by the Federal Communications Commission concerning intrastate telephone service.[18] These cases appear to have been important enough to have warranted the attention of the full courts. It is hard to imagine why they were relegated to panels.

The problems with the Nebraska judicial system are obvious. The state is in need of an intermediate appellate court, and the supreme court needs to be granted some control over its own docket. The current panel system cannot be regarded as an adequate substitute for an

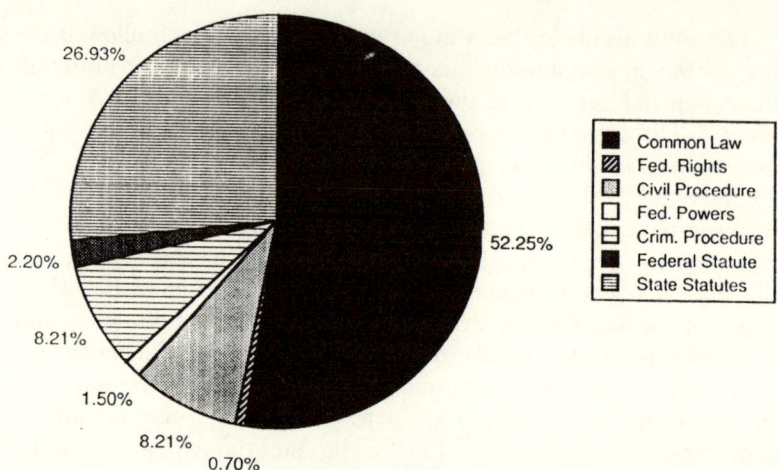

Figure 5.7 Issues in Nebraska Supreme Court, 1975 (Panel Cases Only)

intermediate appellate tier of courts. The panel system does not substantially reduce the workload of the justices, and the system allows for the unusual, and perhaps unseemly, situation in which a justice can sit in review of his or her own panel decisions.

NEW JERSEY: A CLASS IV STATE

New Jersey, like California, possesses an internal unity score of eight, which suggests that the state may have some difficulty resisting federal domination of state politics. However, like California, New Jersey was one of the most activist state courts. The major source of internal unity in the state, according to Elazar, should be the resolution of metropolitan problems, and, indeed, a number of important cases appeared in the docket of the New Jersey Supreme Court that illustrate the importance of this issue. The court considered landlord-tenant relations,[19] the problem of exclusionary zoning,[20] the definition of compensable takings in urban renewal projects,[21] and the constitutionality of municipal rent-control ordinances. So, while the low internal unity of New Jersey did little to explain state supreme court activism, metropolitan problems did appear to influence the issues appearing in the state court's docket.

The judicial system of New Jersey exhibited a number of institutional characteristics consistent with an Individualistic political culture. Justices of the supreme court were well paid—earning $48,000—and well supplied with secretarial and clerical assistance. The legislature authorized fifteen law clerks, ten secretaries, and sixteen additional clerks and librarians to assist the court in 1975. The justices were selected by a partisan method of formal recruitment: gubernatorial appointment with senate advice and consent. However, the state scored only a six on the judicial professionalism scale, two points lower than the national average. This is an unanticipated finding for an Individualistic political culture.

According to the model developed in Chapter 1, states dominated by an Individualistic political culture should possess large, highly bureaucratized court systems. This hypothesis certainly holds true in New Jersey, where the supreme court has traditionally taken an active role in the administration and supervision of the large bench and bar in the state. Glick and Vines (1969) believe that the activist propensity of the New Jersey Supreme Court can be traced to the efforts of former Chief Justice Arthur Vanderbilt, who believed courts should have an important influence on policymaking, lobbied for judicial reform, especially a unified court system, and was an important participant in the framing of New Jersey's 1947 constitution. The justices of the supreme court in 1975 were active in the regulation of the members of the bench and the bar: the court considered seventeen cases involving attorney or judicial discipline. This figure represents 27.4 percent of all cases involving state regulatory statutes.[22]

Some of the expectations concerning the influence of political culture on litigation and court opinions seems to have been met in New Jersey. There was a good fraction of private economic cases heard in the supreme court: 43.6 percent of all common law decisions concerned torts or contracts (see Figure 5.8). There were also more cases involving state regulatory statutes, 34.4 percent of all issues raised, in the New Jersey court than any of the other five courts. Disputes concerning administrative law, commercial regulation and zoning appeared most frequently among the state statutory cases.[23] The justices considered a relatively high fraction of cases involving civil rights and liberties. In fact, the New Jersey court was second only to California in the deliberation of state and federal constitutional rights. Finally, there was a relatively high rate of dissent on the court, although in no

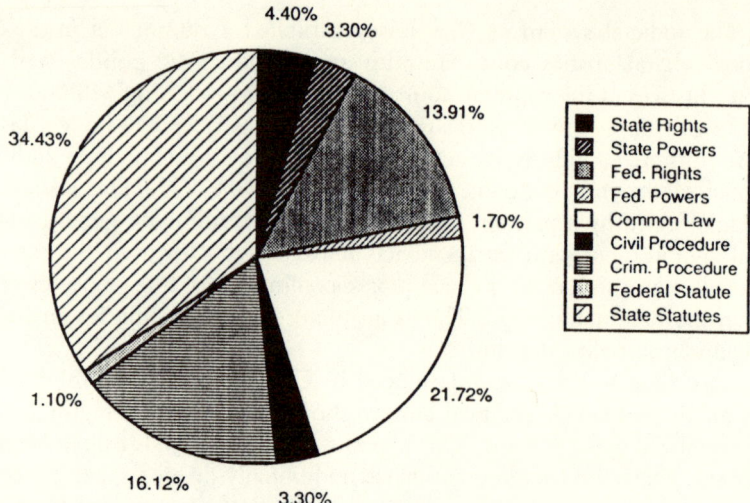

Figure 5.8 Issues in New Jersey Supreme Court, 1975

instance did the level of dissent reach that of Moralistic Michigan, where, theoretically, dissent rates should be low.

The opinions of the New Jersey Supreme Court were generally well crafted and sensitive to the policy needs of the state. The court drew from a wide variety of legal periodicals to help support its reasoning and frequently looked to the courts of last resort of New York and California for guidance. The court also was very willing to make law in the absence of legislative action. For example, in 1973, the supreme court decided *Robinson v. Cahill*, 62 N.J. 473, 303 A.2d 273, which invoked the obscure "thorough and efficient education" clause of the state constitution to require the legislature to enact an equitable system of funding public schools. By 1975, the legislature had failed to develop new means of financing the schools. So, in a reprise of *Robinson v. Cahill*, 67 N.J. 333, 339 A.2d 193, the court indicated its willingness to fashion remedies for the constitutional violation. Speaking through Chief Justice Hughes, the court decided:

> The need for immediate and affirmative action at this juncture is apparent, when one considers the confrontation existing between legislative action, or inaction, and constitutional right . . . If, then, the right of children to a thorough and efficient system of education is a fundamental right guaranteed

by the Constitution, as we have already determined, it follows that the court must "afford an appropriate remedy to address the violation of those rights. To find otherwise would be to say that our Constitution embodies rights in a vacuum, existing only on paper."[24]

The case of *State v. Krol*, 68 N.J. 236, 344 A.2d 289, challenged a section of the New Jersey criminal statutes which required criminals acquitted by reason of insanity to remain committed to a state institution until restored to reason. The court ruled this provision an unconstitutional violation of due process and equal protection because the justices could find no rational basis for distinguishing between criminal and civil commitment standards. In order to fill the gap in criminal procedure made by this exercise of judicial review, the justices took it upon themselves to formulate "constitutional and workable standards." Therefore, the court held:

Commitment requires that there be a substantial risk of dangerous conduct within the reasonably foreseeable future. Evaluation of the magnitude of the risk involves consideration both of the likelihood of dangerous conduct and the seriousness of the harm which may ensue if such conduct takes place.[25]

The court also urged judges to take full advantage of expert testimony in the evaluation of risk and to weigh carefully societal interest in safety against personal autonomy. Both *Robinson v. Cahill* and *State v. Krol* are illustrative of the scope of the role of policymakers that the justices of the New Jersey Supreme Court were willing to play.

The court considered a number of cases which presented important questions for the most densely populated state in the Union and located between the metropolitan centers of New York City and Philadelphia. In response to the growing problems of solid waste management, the New Jersey legislature enacted the Waste Control Act, and, under authority granted in the act, the State Department of Environmental Protection promulgated regulations which banned out-of-state waste from New Jersey landfills. These regulations were challenged as an unconstitutional usurpation of federal commerce authority and as preempted by federal statute. Despite these arguments, in *Hackensack Meadowlands v. Municipal Landfill Authority*, 68 N.J. 451, 348 A.2d 505, the supreme court upheld the state regulations in a unanimous opinion which noted the lack of specific federal regulation in this area and the dominance of the state interest.[26] The supreme court decided another series of cases which addressed the housing problems of the economically disadvantaged. In *South Burlington County N.A.A.C.P. v. Township of Mount Laurel*, 67 N.J. 151, 336 A.2d 713, the court struck down an exclusionary zoning ordinance by reasoning that the general state police power imposes an affirmative duty on the state to legislate for the general welfare, in this case the creation of a certain amount of "least cost" housing. The court upheld rent control ordinances, despite substantive due process challenges,[27] and also formulated criteria by which courts can evaluate whether a rent control ordinance meets reasonableness standards and guarantees a "just and reasonable" profit for the landlord.[28] Finally, the justices expanded the definition of a compensable taking under the federal and state constitutions to encompass the losses suffered by a business when, as part of an urban renewal project which was ultimately abandoned, nearby property was merely threatened with condemnation.[29]

The New Jersey Supreme Court is a sterling example of a good, activist-oriented supreme court. There are a number of factors which probably contributed to the court's performance. Like the California Supreme Court, the New Jersey court was well supplied with clerical and secretarial help which enhanced the research capability of the court. Like California, the New Jersey court had the benefit of an intermediate appellate screening of cases and substantial discretion in choosing cases for review. The New Jersey justices were very willing to use this discretion in 1975: the court decided only 103 cases with full opinion, the lowest figure for any of the courts studied. The ability of the court to limit its docket to the most important cases allows the justices to devote enough time to each case to render a well-crafted, politically sensitive opinion.

There is also an intangible factor which probably contributes to the New Jersey Supreme Court's traditional activism, and that is the heritage of judicial involvement in state politics. Since the tenure of Arthur Vanderbilt, the justices have taken an active role in the administration of the judiciary and court reform. The large number of attorney discipline cases and the efforts of Chief Justice Hughes to urge the creation of a unified system of trial courts via state constitutional amendment are illustrative of the point. While such a political tradition is impossible to quantify, it should be evaluated along with more measurable factors, such as law clerks and court structure, in the attempt to explain judicial activism.

NOTES

1. The class numbers indicate the state court's classification based upon the system developed in Chapter 2.

2. The Arizona Supreme Court reluctantly held that in light of the United States Supreme Court's holdings in *Snaidach v. Family Finance Corp.*, 395 U.S. 337, 89 S.Ct. 1820, 23 L.Ed.2d 349 (1969), and *Fuentes v. Shevlin*, 407 U.S. 67, 92 S.Ct. 1820, 32 L.Ed.2d 556 (1972), the state replevin statute must fail because the statute failed to provide for an independent judicial determination for issuing a writ to seize the property in question or an immediate hearing to determine the possession of the property.

3. See: *People v. Norman*, 14 Ca.3d 929, 123 Cal. Rptr. 109, 538 P.2d 237, and *People v. Longwill*, 14 Ca.3d 943, 123 Cal. Rptr. 297, 538 P.2d 753.

4. See: Powell, Lee, ed. 1980. *Court Reform in Seven States*. National Center for State Courts: Publication No. 50054.

5. *Heilman v. Snyder*, 520 S.W.2d 321.

6. A statement on the Michigan Supreme Court's approach to advisory opinions may be found in *Request for Advisory Opinion of 1975 P.A. 227*, 395 Mich. 148, 235 N.W.2d 321, and in *Request for Advisory Opinion on Constitutionality of 1975 P.A. 195, 196*, 395 Mich. 642, 236 N.W.2d 62.

7. See: *Smookler v. Wheatfield Township*, 394 Mich. 574, 232 N.W.2d 616; *Sabo v. Monroe Township*, 394 Mich. 531, 232 N.W.2d 584; *Nickola v. Grand Blanc Township*, 394 Mich. 589, 232 N.W.2d 616. In *Smookler*, the court cited favorably the arguments and holding of the Pennsylvania Supreme Court in *National Land and Investment Co. v. Eastown Board of Adjustment*, 419 Pa. 504 (1965).

8. *Dearborn Firefighters Union Local No. 412 I.A.F.F.N. v. City of Dearborn*, 394 Mich. 229, 231 N.W.2d 226.

9. *Kube v. Kube*, 193 Neb. 559, 227 N.W.2d 860.

10. *Meyer v. State Farm Mutual Auto Insurance Co.*, 192 Neb. 831, 841; 224 N.W.2d 770.

11. The district court in Nebraska is the trial court of general jurisdiction.

12. See: *State v. Svitak*, 193 Neb. 660, 228 N.W.2d 306.

13. *State v. Simants*, 194 Neb. 783, 790; 236 N.W.2d 794. The decision was reversed by the United States Supreme Court in *Nebraska Press Ass'n v. Stuart*, 427 U.S. 539, 96 S.Ct. 2791, 49 L.Ed.2d 683.

14. *State v. Holmberg*, 194 Neb. 337, 231 N.W.2d 672.

15. *Botsch v. Reisdorff,* 193 Neb. 165, 226 N.W.2d 121; *Gertsch v. Gerber,* 193 Neb. 181, 226 N.W.2d 132; *Lubash v. Langmeier,* 193 Neb. 371, 227 N.W.2d 405.

16. *Williams v. Nebraska City Airport Authority,* 193 Neb. 567, 228 N.W.2d 276.

17. *State ex rel. Meyer v. American Community Stores Corp.,* 193 Neb. 634, 228 N.W.2d 299.

18. *Sherdon v. Dann,* 193 Neb. 769, 229 N.W.2d 531.

19. *Braitman v. Overlook Terrace Corp.,* 68 N.J. 368, 346 A.2d 76.

20. *South Burlington County N.A.A.C.P. v. Township of Mount Laurel,* 67 N.J. 151, 336 A.2d 713.

21. *Washington Market Enterprises v. Trenton,* 68 N.J. 107, 343 A.2d 408.

22. *Troy Hills Village v. Parsippany-Troy Hills Township Council,* 68 N.J. 605, 350 A.2d 34; *Hutton Park Gardens v. West Orange Town Council,* 68 N.J. 543, 350 A.2d 1; *Burnette v. Borough of New Milford,* 68 N.J. 576, 350 A.2d 19.

23. It should be noted that the California Supreme Court also was heavily involved with the regulation of the lower courts and legal professionals in the state. In 1975, the California court heard twenty-seven cases involving attorney or judicial discipline. This number represents 32.5 percent of all state regulatory statute cases.

24. *Robinson v. Cahill,* 67 N.J. 333, 346–7; 351 A.2d 713.

25. *State v. Krol,* 68 N.J. 236, 260; 344 A.2d 289, 302.

26. The New Jersey court was ultimately reversed by the United States Supreme Court in *Philadelphia v. New Jersey,* 430 U.S. 141, 97 S.Ct. 987, 51 L.Ed.2d 224 (1977).

27. See *Hutton Park Gardens.*

28. *Troy Hills Village.* According to Justice Pashman, who wrote for the court, the allowable rent

must be high enough to encourage good management including adequate maintenance of services, to furnish a reward for efficiency, to discourage the flight of capital from the rental housing market, and to enable operators to maintain and support their credit. A just and reasonable return is one which is not so high as to defeat the purposes of rent control nor permit landlords to demand of tenants more than the fair value of the property and services which are provided. (68 N.J. 604, 629)

29. *Washington Market Enterprises v. Trenton.* The New Jersey Supreme Court believed this to have been a narrow holding compared with the California Supreme Court decision in *Klopping v. City of Whittier,* 8 Ca.3d 39, 104 Cal. Rptr. 1, 500 P.2d 1345 (1972).

6. Conclusions

This book was a preliminary effort to add to our knowledge of state supreme court performance. An attempt was made to identify some measures of supreme court performance—a judicial activism score, reversal and dissent rates—and to explain variation in performances in terms of contextual and institutional variables. These independent variables, such as political culture and the structure of the state judicial system, were derived from the findings of numerous researchers and placed in a model which provides a framework for the systematic studies of state courts of last resort. I have attempted to test the utility of some of the aspects of the models through a quantitative study of state judicial systems, the social and political backgrounds of justices, and the work of six supreme courts. This final chapter is devoted to an evaluation of the strengths and weaknesses of the model in light of the quantitative findings.

According to Elazar (1966), states with high internal unity will be best equipped to fend off federal encroachment on their policies. However, only limited support for this hypothesis was found in the limited study of six courts. Highly unified states, such as Nebraska and Arizona, rarely invoked independent and adequate state grounds in constitutional cases, while diversified states, such as Michigan and New Jersey, more frequently relied exclusively upon state law. Moreover, there was little evidence of Elazar's sources of internal unity in the dockets of the supreme courts. There were only three disputes over the allocation of water resources in the combined dockets of California and Arizona, although there was some evidence of the importance of metropolitan problems in New Jersey, economic development in

Michigan and agriculture in Nebraska. While internal unity may be a poor predictor of the use of independent and adequate state grounds by a state supreme court, or the appearance of certain issues important to state politics in the dockets of the courts, the concept may fare a little better in the prediction of dissent rates. Generally, the lower the state's internal unity, the more likely dissent will appear on the supreme court. This point is best illustrated by the case of Michigan in which the conflictual nature of state politics is reflected in the disagreement among the justices along party lines.

The failure of the concept of internal unity to account for much variation in supreme court performance may be due to a number of factors. Bear in mind that any preliminary assessment of the utility of any of these variables is primarily impressionistic, based upon a qualitative examination of the work of the courts for a single year. It is possible that a systematic relationship between internal unity and judicial activism, dissents and the nature of issues appearing on the docket, may emerge in a comprehensive multi-year study. Another possibility could be the existence of distinctly judicial sources of internal unity. Elazar speaks of a single, overriding issue that has become the rallying point for all state politics, but this conception of internal unity may be too broad for application to the state's judicial systems with its own special problems. For example, the allocation of scarce water resources may be crucial to the people in Arizona, but for the Arizona state judiciary, the overriding concern is the disposition of numerous criminal cases arising from Mexican smuggling operations. Consequently, Arizona courts are concerned with the appropriate balance between the rights of criminal defendants embodied in the federal and state constitutions and the need of society to curb criminal activity. Because of the importance of this problem to the administration of justice in Arizona, it is reasonable to expect a good deal of judicial creativity in this area. However, as indicated in earlier chapters, the crime control decisions of the United States Supreme Court under the leadership of Chief Justice Warren Burger are perceived by the Arizona justices as ideally suited to the needs of the state. Hence, there is no incentive for the Arizona court to resort to novel interpretations of the state constitution in the area of criminal justice. This limited investigation of state supreme courts does not allow for the identification of uniquely judicial sources of internal unity, but this may be a fertile area for future study.

Conclusions

Elazar's concept of political culture was another contextual variable incorporated into the model of factors related to state supreme court performance. Political culture helps to define the role of government in a state and forms which governmental institutions and practices should assume. This research has shown some relationship between political culture, indicated by geographic region, and certain institutional characteristics of the state judiciary, but the relationships were imperfect. The strongest relationships found existed between political culture and methods of formal judicial recruitment. The best example of the relationship between political culture and judicial politics may be seen in the case of Traditionalistic Kentucky and citizen resistance to the modernization of the state court system.

Future studies may show a decreased relationship between political culture and institutional characteristics of a state's judicial system. Efforts to modernize and streamline court systems in the interest of efficiency have become more common, and most state systems now embody some elements of the American Bar Association's model state judicial system. By 1977, more than two-thirds of the states maintained intermediate appellate courts and judicial qualifications commissions. Furthermore, a number of states recently have discarded partisan or nonpartisan elections as a means of formal recruitment in favor of some variation on the Missouri Plan. If this trend toward the standardization of the state judicial systems continues, any relationship between political culture and judicial institutions may soon be extinguished. For example, in 1975, the Kentucky court system fit squarely within the Traditionalistic model, but, by 1977, after the passage of new legislation reorganizing the courts, the Kentucky system more closely approximated the simple, centrally administered court system of an Individualistic culture.

Political culture, then, may one day cease to be a useful predictor of the institutional features of the state judicial systems. The concept also did little to explain dissent rates, where it was hypothesized that dissent rates should be highest in courts in states dominated by the Individualistic culture. Here, the justices of Moralistic Michigan consistently showed higher dissent rates than any other state, including Individualistic New Jersey. Again, however, it would be wrong to completely discard the variable given the preliminary nature of this work.

The scholarly literature has suggested that institutional variables, notably formal recruitment plans, should be related to the social and political backgrounds of supreme court justices. However, this research has revealed no statistically significant relationships were found between judicial backgrounds and a number of institutional variables: method of formal recruitment, the use of a merit plan or term of office. Some researchers have suggested that the effectiveness of elections in recruiting a particular kind of legal talent for the bench has been diminished by the interim appointment power of the governor. However, no statistically significant relationships were found between interim appointees and justices who came to the bench via the formal recruitment process. Some significant differences in judicial backgrounds were found by geographic region. These differences may be interpreted as an indication of the importance of cultural variables in determining who should or will enter state politics. Political culture, then, may remain important in the recruitment of state political officials, even though the concept may one day be of limited value in the study of the institutional characteristics of state judicial systems.

The failure of different methods of formal recruitment to attract different kinds of individuals to the benches of the state supreme courts can be viewed in terms of the concept of institutionalization. As organizations grow and are required to perform an increased number of tasks, a certain degree of standardization of procedures and officials is necessary for the smooth functioning of the organization. The similarity of the social and political backgrounds of the state supreme court justices may be seen as a manifestation of one element of the process of institutionalization, the standardization of backgrounds and career patterns for state judicial officers.

Institutionalization, or what some alternatively may call "bureaucratization," is also necessary to preserve the independent status of an organization and to prevent the encroachment of rival organizations on its territory. While courts retain a monopoly on the administration of justice, they are dependent on other branches of state government for funding, for the regulation of the structure of the judicial system, for the definition of large parts of their jurisdiction, for the enforcement of their decisions and, in some states, for the selection of judges. State courts, then, are always in danger of losing their independence to other branches of the state government. One way in which state supreme courts can preserve the autonomy of the judiciary is by taking an active role in the administration and supervision of the bench and

Conclusions

the bar. Chief Justice James Duke Cameron of Arizona (1977), a jurist who generally urges judicial restraint, believes that the one acceptable area for state court activism is the administration of the judicial system. He argues that such activism is a necessary requirement of the doctrine of separation of powers. According to Cameron, there are three major concerns in state judicial administration: the promulgation of rules governing the operation of the court system, the control of admission to the bar and the exercise of continuing supervision and discipline, or, discipline and removal of members of the judiciary who become disabled or are guilty of misconduct. This work with state supreme courts has indicated that the New Jersey and California courts are most active in the administration of justice. Perhaps this exercise of responsibility for the internal supervision of the state judiciary can be seen as another facet of institutionalization.

While contextual variables appeared to be of limited utility in explaining variations in court performance, institutional variables and norms are perhaps better predictors of decision-making activity. The presence of an intermediate appellate court should be related to increased dissent rates and increased reversals of lower court decisions. It can be argued further than an intermediate appellate court should increase the judicial activism score of state supreme court opinions. Under the scoring system used for judicial activism, up to six points are awarded for the citation of law review articles and sister state precedents. The intermediate appellate court screening of cases should decrease the number of cases to be decided by the supreme court, thus allowing more time to be devoted to each decision. This additional time available for research should translate into better-crafted opinions with numerous citations to support the legal reasoning underlying the decision, and, by the definition of the activism score, the more citations, the higher the score. The amount of discretion granted to a state supreme court in selecting cases for review will also be related to dissents, reversals and judicial activism: the greater the discretion, the greater the number of dissents, reversals and activism score. The high dissent and reversal rates would be the result of the selection of novel or problematic cases for review; the increased activism score would be the product of the increased time for research.

Variations in dissent rates may be the function of different decision-making norms on state supreme courts. This hypothesis drew on Sickels' (1965) study of the Maryland Court of Appeals and Fenno's (1973) study of committees in the United States House of Representatives. In states such as Kentucky, Nebraska and Arizona, the dominant norm appears to be that of agreement whenever possible; consequently, the justices may logroll to reach the desired consensus. Other states, such as Michigan, may operate under an expectation of partisan disagreement, and, therefore, no effort will be made to secure a single opinion for the court. The fact that highly partisan courts seldom speak with one voice ultimately may be detrimental to the courts' effectiveness in state politics since the law is never settled and may change as soon as the next judicial election. Finally, courts such as those of New Jersey and California may attempt to minimize public conflict among the justices whenever possible in an effort to increase the strength of the court's pronouncements, thereby maximizing the influence of the court in state government. The verification of the existence of these decision-making norms is beyond the scope of this book.

My work here allows me to make some recommendations for the improvement of state supreme courts. Bear in mind here that I favor an activist—or law-making—role for the state judiciary. In addition, I believe that the development of a uniquely state-derived body of constitutional law is an important contribution to not only federalism but the enhanced protection of civil rights and liberties.

While all formal recruitment plans seem to bring similar individuals to the benches of the supreme courts, each plan is not of equal value. I favor any appointed method of formal recruitment over any elected method. An appointed system allows candidates for judicial office to be interviewed and evaluated by knowledgeable political elites who are aware of the power and importance of judicial office. Furthermore, a civil libertarian-minded governor could question a candidate on his or her willingness to invoke independent and adequate state grounds as a means of providing special protection for the rights and liberties of the people of the state. A realistic view of judicial election shows that the average American voter has minimal levels of information on candidates for judgeships, and in light of low information levels, the general lack of interest in judicial elections, popular election of judges is a far less than ideal means of formal recruitment.

I favor long terms of office for justices of appellate courts. Most American are firm believers in the desirability of an independent judiciary that is sufficiently insulated from majoritarian pressures to render decisions protective of minority rights. It is no accident that the

Conclusions

most civil libertarian courts in this study, California and New Jersey, are also the states with the longest terms of office for their supreme court justices.

This study of six courts pointed out some obvious areas of improvement for state supreme courts. Examination of Kentucky and Nebraska showed the importance of an intermediate appellate court and, especially in the case of Nebraska, the need for discretionary review by the supreme court. The creation of panels within a supreme court is not an adequate substitute for an intermediate appellate court. The use of panels, when an intermediate appellate court is in operation, as in Arizona, is a wasteful practice. The creation of an intermediate tier of courts and the granting of the power of discretionary review to the supreme court are probably the two most important reforms that can be introduced into a state court system.

A final assessment of state supreme courts holds that levels of state court activism were generally quite low in 1975. There are a number of possible explanations for the infrequent use of independent and adequate state grounds. For years state supreme courts have worked in the shadow of the United States Supreme Court. From 1937 to the 1970s, the trend in American constitutional law was toward federal domination in areas as diverse as economic regulation and individual rights. Litigants regarded state supreme courts as a poor second choice to the federal courts in civil rights litigation, and few attorneys thought to look to long, unused provisions of obscure state constitutions. As G. Alan Tarr (1982) has emphasized, state courts are legally subservient to the United States Supreme Court in the interpretation of federal law. Although Tarr has found some evidence of non-compliance by state supreme courts, these evasive decisions were few and far between. In this study, there were few examples of the use of state constitutional analogs to the federal Bill of Rights to enhance the protection of individual rights and liberties. It is possible that the state supreme courts are reluctant to invoke state constitutional provisions which are similar in language to federal provisions because of the difficulties in justifying different interpretatons with different outcomes for similarly worded constitutional provisions.[1] The work of some state courts is made easier by the presence in some state constitutions of clauses which distinguish state guaranteed rights from federally guaranteed rights, as in California. However, the real potential for state court creativity probably lies in the interpretation of state constitutional provisions with no federal counterpart. The "thorough and efficient education" guaranteed in the New Jersey constitution, the explicit right to privacy in Alaska, the guarantee of a secret ballot in Michigan, a right to appeal in Arizona are but a few examples of unique provisions in state constitutions which can be interpreted without reference to federal law. These uniquely state-derived guarantees of individual rights and liberties may ultimately provide the material for future creative state supreme court constitutional interpretation.

NOTE

1. For some suggestions as to how state supreme courts can justify different reading of state constitutional analogs to the federal Bill of Rights, see: Note. 1977. The New Federalism: Toward a Principled Interpretation of the State Constitution. *Stanford Law Review*, 29:297–321.

Appendix

Table A.1 Factor Loadings: Rotated Factor Matrix, 1976, 1978

1976

Variable	Factor Loadings	
	Factor 1	Factor 2
Technical and Clerical Support	0.72344	0.20379
Types Trial Courts	-0.01422	0.26899
Types Limited Courts	0.13435	0.66179
Judges Intermediate Appellate Courts	0.87122	0.21791
Judges Trial Courts	0.89228	-0.21420
Term of Office	0.08143	0.24161
Salary	0.72410	0.24943

(required 22 iterations)

1978

Variable	Factor 1	Factor 2	Factor 3
Technical and Clerical Support	0.79220	-0.03506	0.31707
Types Trial Courts	-0.02007	0.25157	0.07300
Types Limited Courts	0.10595	0.86828	0.11544
Judges Intermediate Appellate Courts	0.89356	0.19526	-0.13621
Judges Trial Courts	0.88497		0.35812
Term of Office	0.00085	0.12701	0.35812
Salary	0.72467	0.17384	0.52632

(required more than 25 iterations)

Table A.2 Formal Recruitment and Judicial Backgrounds, 1975, 1977[1]

Variable	1975								1977							
	N=38 Appointment		N=57 Mixed		N=67 Non-Partisan Election		N=83 Partisan Election		N=44 Appointment		N=81 Mixed		N=69 Non-Partisan Election		N=76 Partisan Election	
	N	%	N	%	N	%	N	%	N	%	N	%	N	%	N	%
Prior Judicial Experience	30	81.1	35	62.5	45	67.2	53	63.9	31	70.5	50	62.5	46	66.7	48	63.2
Sex																
Female	0	0.0	0	0.0	1	1.5	3	3.6	1	2.3	2	2.5	3	4.3	3	3.9
Male	37	100.0	57	100.0	66	98.5	80	96.4	43	97.7	79	97.5	66	95.7	73	96.1
Race																
White	34	97.1	57	100.0	67	100.0	83	100.0	41	97.6	79	97.5	67	97.1	76	100.0
Black	1	2.9	0	0.0	0	0.0	0	0.0	1	2.4	2	2.5	2	2.9	0	0.0
Previous Political Activity	20	52.6	17	29.8	30	44.8	42	50.6	20	45.5	30	37.0	31	44.9	33	43.4
Political Party																
Democratic	7	43.8	13	48.1	16	72.7	41	100.0	10	52.6	17	47.2	22	84.6	43	100.0
Republican	8	50.0	13	48.1	6	27.3	0	0.0(**S)	8	42.1	18	50.0	4	15.4	0	0.0(**S)
Independent	1	6.3	1	3.7	0	5.7	0	0.0(*)	1	5.3	1	2.8	0	0.0	0	0.0
Attended In-State College	16	47.1	34	68.0	46	82.1	61	79.2(*)	21	51.2	47	64.4	46	76.7	60	84.5(*)
Attended Ivy League College	10	29.4	5	10.0	2	3.6	6	7.8(**S)	11	26.8	7	9.6	4	6.7	5	7.0(**)
Attended In-State Law School	14	37.8	39	69.6	48	72.7	62	74.7(*)	19	43.2	54	67.5	48	70.6	53	70.7(*)

	N	%	N	%	N	%	N	%	N	%	N	%	N	%	N	%
Attended Ivy League Law School	12	32.4	6	10.7	8	12.1	12	14.5(*S)	18	40.9	11	13.8	7	10.3	11	14.7(*)
Born In-State	27	79.4	36	64.3	54	83.1	74	89.2(*)	34	81.0	53	66.3	51	77.3	66	89.2(*)
Birthplace Size																
Urban	15	45.5	19	33.9	26	40.6	23	27.7	22	53.7	27	33.8	23	36.5	18	24.3
Small Town	17	51.5	35	62.5	37	57.8	52	62.7	18	43.9	51	63.8	36	57.1	49	66.2
Rural	1	3.0	2	3.6	1	1.6	8	9.6	1	2.4	2	2.5	4	6.3	7	9.5
Religion																
Protestant	10	45.5	34	79.1	34	73.9	56	80.0	11	39.3	46	73.0	31	75.6	51	81.0
Jewish	1	4.5	2	4.7	1	2.2	4	5.7	3	10.7	3	4.8	0	0.0	2	3.2
Catholic	9	40.9	4	9.3	10	21.7	10	14.3	11	39.3	9	14.3	10	24.4	9	14.3(**)
Other	2	9.1	3	7.0	1	2.2	0	0.0	3	10.7	5	7.9	0	0.0	1	1.6
Additional Study	1	2.6	7	12.3	12	17.9	8	9.6	3	6.8	10	12.3	12	17.4	7	9.2
Held Elected Political Office	17	44.7	12	22.8	20	29.9	30	36.1	17	38.6	22	27.2	18	26.1	24	31.6
Prosecutorial Experience	15	39.5	36	63.2	27	40.3	35	42.2(*)	14	31.8	47	58.0	25	36.2	35	46.1(*)
Military Service	21	55.3	32	56.1	41	61.2	55	66.3	27	61.4	51	63.0	39	56.5	52	68.4
Primary Pre-Supreme Court Career																
Law Professor	2	5.7	3	5.3	0	0.0	5	6.0	5	11.4	3	3.8	2	2.9	5	6.6
Judge	16	45.7	25	43.9	26	38.8	37	44.6	16	36.4	34	42.5	30	44.1	33	43.4

Table A.2 (continued)

					1975									1977			
Variable	N=38 Appointment		N=57 Mixed		N=67 Non-Partisan Election		N=83 Partisan Election		N=44 Appointment		N=81 Mixed		N=69 Non-Partisan Election		N=76 Partisan Election	
	N	%	N	%	N	%	N	%	N	%	N	%	N	%	N	%
Practicing Attorney	13	37.1	20	35.1	27	40.3	28	33.7	19	43.2	26	32.5	25	36.8	25	32.9
Prosecutor	4	11.4	9	15.8	9	13.4	9	10.8	4	9.1	14	17.5	7	10.3	6	7.9
Elected Official	0	0.0	0	0.0	3	4.5	3	3.8	0	0.0	1	1.3	3	4.4	6	7.9
Other Politics	0	0.0	0	0.0	1	1.5	0	0.0	0	0.0	2	2.5	0	0.0	0	0.0
Business	0	0.0	0	0.0	0	0.0	1	1.2	0	0.0	0	0.0	0	0.0	1	1.3
Law Enforcement	0	0.0	0	0.0	0	0.0	0	0.0	0	0.0	0	0.0	0	0.0	0	0.0
Military	0	0.0	0	0.0	1	1.5	0	0.0	0	0.0	0	0.0	1	1.5	0	0.0
Religious Status																
High Status Protestants	9	40.9	20	46.5	25	54.3	23	32.9	10	35.7	27	43.5	20	48.8	20	31.7
Low Status Protestants	1	4.5	12	27.9	9	19.6	33	37.1(*)	7	3.6	16	25.8	10	25.8	31	49.7(*)
Catholics																
Jews	12	54.5	11	25.6	12	26.1	14	20.0	17	60.7	19	30.6	11	30.6	12	19.0
Localism																
All In-State	5	16.1	21	43.8	30	55.6	45	58.4(*)	8	20.5	31	43.7	30	51.7	42	60.0(*)

Average Years Judicial Experience (all)	X̄=9.9	X̄=6.9	X̄=6.3	X̄=7.0	X̄=8.4	X̄=6.7	X̄=6.8	X̄=6.8
Average Years Judicial Experience (those with)	X̄=12.5	X̄=11.3	X̄=9.7	X̄=12.0	X̄=11.9	X̄=10.8	X̄=10.3	X̄=11.2
Age at Elevation to State Supreme Court	X̄=53.7	X̄=51.9	X̄=50.0	X̄=52.8	X̄=53.7	X̄=51.0	X̄=51.0	X̄=52.3
Tenure on State Supreme Court (years)	X̄=9.9	X̄=7.6	X̄=6.7	X̄=8.3	X̄=8.6	X̄=8.5	X̄=6.7	X̄=9.2

[1]The four formal recruitment processes are defined as follows: "Appointment" - gubernatorial appointment with or without "merit" list. "Mixed" - initial gubernatorial appointment with or without a "merit" list with the requirement of a retention election on the justices' record. "Non-partisan Election" - popular election with primary labels on ballot.

Please see table 3.1 for an explanation of the variables and the tests of statistical significance. One asterisk (*) indicates the results are statistically significant at the 0.05 level or better. Two asterisks (**) indicate the results are significant at the 0.01 level or better, however, these results should be interpreted with caution due to the problem of expected cell frequencies of less than five in the calculation of the chi-square value. Asterisks enclosed within parentheses indicate the results are no longer statistically significant when controls for geographic regions are introduced. Letters beside asterisks indicate particular regions in which the relationship remains statistically significant: N = North, S = South, M = Midwest, W = West.

Table A.3 Regional Variations in Judicial Backgrounds, 1975, 1977[1]

	1975								1977							
	North		South		Midwest		West		North		South		Midwest		West	
Variable	N	%	N	%	N	%	N	%	N	%	N	%	N	%	N	%
Prior Judicial Experience	30	75.0	55	61.1	48	71.6	30	65.2	35	69.4	54	62.1	51	66.2	36	64.3
Sex																
Female	0	0.0	3	3.3	1	1.5	0	0.0	1	2.0	3	3.4	4	5.2	1	1.8
Male	40	100.0	88	96.7	66	98.5	46	100.0	48	98.0	85	96.6	73	94.8	55	98.2
Race																
White	40	100.0	90	98.9	67	100.0	46	100.0	48	98.0	88	100.0	75	97.4	52	96.3
Black	0	0.0	1	1.1	0	0.0	0	0.0	1	2.0	0	0.0	2	2.6	2	3.7
Previous Political Activity	23	56.1	47	51.6	23	34.3	16	34.8*	25	51.0	43	48.9	24	31.2	22	39.3
Political Party																
Democratic	7	58.3	48	90.6	10	43.5	12	66.7	8	50.0	50	92.6	15	51.7	19	76.0
Republican	4	33.3	5	9.4	13	56.5	5	27.8**	7	43.8	4	7.4	14	48.3	5	20.0**
Independent	1	8.3	0	0.0	0	0.0	1	5.6	1	6.3	0	0.0	0	0.0	1	4.0
Attended In-State College	20	52.6	66	82.5	45	75.0	26	66.7*	24	52.2	68	85.0	51	72.9	31	63.3*
Attended Ivy League College	13	34.2	4	5.0	2	3.3	4	10.3*	16	34.8	2	2.5	4	5.7	5	10.2*
Attended In-State Law School	14	35.0	75	83.3	50	75.8	24	52.2*	19	38.8	69	79.3	57	76.0	29	51.8*

	N	%	N	%	N	%	N	%	N	%	N	%	N	%	N	%
Attended Ivy League Law School	18	45.0	6	6.7	7	10.6	7	15.2*	26	53.1	4	4.6	8	10.7	9	16.1*
Born In-State	34	89.5	77	85.6	56	84.8	24	54.5*	41	85.4	73	84.9	61	82.4	29	53.7*
Birthplace Size																
Urban	23	60.5	19	21.1	22	33.8	19	44.2	27	56.3	19	22.1	24	33.3	20	38.5
Small Town	15	39.5	63	70.0	41	63.1	22	51.2**	21	43.8	57	66.3	46	63.9	30	57.7
Rural	0	0.0	8	8.9	2	3.1	2	4.7	0	0.0	10	11.6	2	2.8	2	3.8
Religion																
Protestant	8	30.8	72	92.3	35	74.5	19	63.3	12	37.5	70	92.1	37	72.5	20	55.6
Jewish	4	15.4	2	2.6	1	2.1	1	3.3	4	12.5	2	2.6	1	2.0	1	2.8
Catholic	14	53.8	4	5.1	10	21.3	5	16.7**	15	46.9	4	5.3	12	23.5	8	22.2**
Other	0	0.0	0	0.0	1	2.1	5	16.7	1	3.1	0	0.0	1	2.0	7	19.4
Additional Study	3	7.3	12	13.2	7	10.4	6	13.0	4	8.2	14	15.9	8	10.4	6	10.7
Held Elected Political Office	14	34.1	31	34.1	22	32.8	13	28.3	16	32.7	28	31.8	24	31.2	13	23.2
Prosecutorial Experience	16	39.0	35	38.5	36	53.7	26	56.5	16	32.7	36	40.9	38	49.4	31	55.4
Military Service	23	56.1	66	72.5	37	55.2	23	50.0*	32	65.3	65	73.9	41	53.2	31	55.4*
Primary Pre-Supreme Court Career																
Law Professor	1	2.5	5	5.6	2	3.0	2	4.4	5	10.2	5	5.7	2	2.6	3	5.6
Judge	22	55.0	35	38.9	33	49.3	14	31.1	23	46.9	36	40.9	41	53.2	13	24.1
Practicing Attorney	14	35.0	36	40.0	22	32.8	16	35.6	17	34.7	34	38.6	23	29.9	21	38.9
Prosecutor	3	7.5	9	10.0	8	11.9	11	24.4	4	8.2	6	6.8	8	10.4	13	24.1

Table A.3 (continued)

	1975								1977							
	North		South		Midwest		West		North		South		Midwest		West	
Variable	N	%	N	%	N	%	N	%	N	%	N	%	N	%	N	%
Elected Official	0	0.0	3	3.3	2	3.0	1	2.2	0	0.0	4	4.5	3	3.9	3	5.6
Other Politics	0	0.0	1	1.1	0	0.0	0	0.0	0	0.0	2	2.3	0	0.0	0	0.0
Business	0	0.0	1	1.1	0	0.0	0	0.0	0	0.0	1	1.1	0	0.0	0	0.0
Law Enforcement	0	0.0	0	0.0	0	0.0	0	0.0	0	0.0	0	0.0	0	0.0	0	0.0
Military	0	0.0	0	0.0	0	0.0	0	0.0	0	0.0	0	0.0	0	0.0	1	1.9
Religious Status																
High Status Protestants	8	30.8	32	41.0	22	46.8	15	50.0	12	37.5	26	34.2	23	46.0	16	44.4
Low Status Protestants	0	0.0	40	51.3	11	23.4	4	4.0*	0	0.0	43	56.6	11	22.0	4	11.1*
Catholics and Jews	18	69.2	6	7.7	14	29.8	11	36.7	20	62.5	7	9.2	16	32.0	16	44.4
Localism																
All In-State	6	16.7	51	65.4	32	55.2	12	31.6*	9	20.0	52	66.7	36	53.7	14	29.2*

Average Years Judicial Experience (all)	X̄=9.6	X̄=6.2	X̄=7.4	X̄=6.9	X̄=8.6	X̄=6.8	X̄=6.8	X̄=6.3
Average Years Judicial Experience (those with)	X̄=14.0	X̄=10.7	X̄=10.6	X̄=11.0	X̄=12.6	X̄=11.2	X̄=10.5	X̄=9.8
Age at Elevation to State Supreme Court	X̄=54.5	X̄=51.4	X̄=52.1	X̄=50.7	X̄=54.1	X̄=51.1	X̄=52.0	X̄=50.8
Tenure on State Supreme Court (years)	X̄=8.4	X̄=8.5	X̄=7.6	X̄=7.9	X̄=8.2	X̄=8.5	X̄=8.7	X̄=9.0

1   See Table 3.1 for an explanation of the variables.

*   One asterisk indicates the results are statistically significant at the 0.05 level or better.

** Two asterisks indicate the results are significant at the 0.01 level or better - however, these results should be interpreted with caution due to the problem of expected frequencies of less than five in the calculation of the chi-square value.

Table A.4 Comparing Interim Appointees and Formally Recruited Justices, 1975, 1977

	1975				1977			
Variable	Formal Recruitment N=149		Interim Appointment N=56		Formal Recruitment N=162		Interim Appointees N=56	
	N	%	N	%	N	%	N	%
Prior Judicial Experience	98	66.2	37	66.1	111	68.9	34	60.7
Sex								
Female	2	1.3	1	1.8	5	3.1	3	5.4
Male	147	98.7	55	98.2	157	96.9	53	94.6
Race								
White	146	99.3	56	100.0	155	96.9	56	100.0
Black	1	0.7	0	0.0	5	3.1	0	0.0
Previous Political Activity	64	43.0	29	51.8	67	41.4	26	46.4
Political Party								
Democratic	49	75.4	19	95.0	60	74.1	20	95.2
Republican	14	21.5	1	5.0	19	23.5	1	4.8
Independent	2	3.1	0	0.0	2	2.5	0	0.0
Attended In-State College	89	66.9	42	87.5(*)	101	68.2	41	82.0
Attended Ivy League College	16	12.0	4	8.3	22	14.9	3	6.0
Attended In-State Law School	98	66.2	39	69.6	103	64.4	36	64.3
Attended Ivy League Law School	98	66.2	39	69.6	103	64.4	36	64.3
Born In-State	117	80.7	48	87.3	124	79.0	43	78.2

Birthplace Size							
Urban	59	41.0	14	25.9	59	38.1	14	26.4
Small Town	80	55.6	34	63.0(*S)	90	58.1	32	60.4(*S)
Rural	5	3.5	6	11.1	6	3.9	7	13.2
Religion								
Protestant	78	70.3	32	84.2	84	71.2	28	82.4
Jewish	6	5.4	2	5.3	5	4.2	1	2.9
Catholic	24	21.6	4	10.5	24	20.3	5	14.7
Other	3	2.7	0	0.0	5	4.2	0	0.0
Additional Study	22	14.8	1	1.8(*)	24	14.8	2	3.6(*)
Held Elected Political Office	48	32.2	15	26.8	44	27.2	14	25.0
Prosecutorial Experience	57	38.3	29	51.8	59	36.4	30	53.6(*N)
Military Service	91	61.1	37	66.1	101	62.3	35	62.5
Served as Chief Justice	36	24.2	12	21.4	36	22.2	10	17.9
Primary Pre-Supreme Court Career								
Law Professor	7	4.7	2	3.6	11	6.8	3	5.5
Judge	66	44.6	25	44.6	72	44.4	23	41.8
Practicing Attorney	50	33.8	20	35.7	51	31.5	21	38.2
Prosecutor	18	12.2	8	14.3	19	11.7	6	10.9

Table A.4 (continued)

Variable	1975				1977			
	Formal Recruitment N=149		Interim Appointment N=56		Formal Recruitment N=162		Interim Appointees N=56	
	N	%	N	%	N	%	N	%
Elected Official	4	2.7	1	1.8	7	4.3	2	3.6
Other Politics	1	0.7	0	0.0	0	0.0	0	0.0
Business	1	0.7	0	0.0	1	0.6	0	0.0
Law Enforcement	0	0.0	0	0.0	0	0.0	0	0.0
Military	1	0.7	0	0.0	1	0.6	0	0.0
Localism All In-State	59	46.1	27	56.3	64	44.8	26	52.0
Regional Breakdown[1]								
North	29	80.6	7	19.4	34	85.0	6	15.0
South	57	69.5	25	30.5	53	71.6	21	28.4
Midwest	37	75.5	12	24.5	45	75.0	15	25.0
West	26	68.4	12	31.6	30	68.2	14	31.8
Religious Status								
High Status Protestant	49	44.1	15	39.5	52	44.4	12	35.3
Low Status Protestant	29	26.1	17	44.7	30	25.6	16	47.1(*)
Catholics	33	29.7	6	15.8	35	29.9	6	17.6
Jews								

Average Years of Judicial Experience (all)	$\bar{X}=7.7$	$\bar{X}=5.6$	$\bar{X}=7.6$	$\bar{X}=5.6$
Average Years of Judicial Experience (those with)	$\bar{X}=11.9$	$\bar{X}=9.8$	$\bar{X}=11.0$	$\bar{X}=9.8$
Age at Elevation to State Supreme Court	$\bar{X}=51.9$	$\bar{X}=52.4$	$\bar{X}=51.7$	$\bar{X}=52.6$
Tenure on State Supreme Court (years)	$\bar{X}=7.6$	$\bar{X}=8.1$	$\bar{X}=8.2$	$\bar{X}=8.8$

NOTE: Please see Table 3.1 for an explanation of the variables.

Differences statistically significant at the 0.05 level or better are noted by an asterisk. T-tests were used to determine the significance of differences between means; chi-square was used to determine the significance of frequency distributions. Discrepancies between N's and percents are due to the exclusion of missing values. Percentages may not total 100% due to rounding error.

[1] Percents are calculated here to reflect the proportion of justices in each region recruited by formal process and interim appointment.

Table A.5 Classification of State Supreme Court Cases

The 100 Series: Federal Constitution
```
100   Supremacy Clause
101   Separation of Powers
102   Qualifications, elections of legislature
103   Salaries: Speech and Debate
104   Powers of the legislature
105   Suspension of habeas corpus
106   No bills of attainder - Congress
107   No ex post facto laws - Congress
108   No export duties on state products
109   No bills of attainder - state
110   No ex post facto laws - state
111   Contract clause
112   Election, qualifications of executive
113   Executive powers
114   Impeachment proceedings
115   Judiciary - judicial power and tenure of judges
116   Judiciary - jurisdiction
117   Definition of the crime of treason
118   Full faith and credit clause
119   Privileges and immunities - state equal footing
120   Rendition
121   Property power of Congress
122   Republican guarantee
123   Amending the constitution
124   First Amendment - Establishment clause
125   First Amendment - Free exercise
126   First Amendment - Free speech/press
127   First Amendment - Assembly
128   First Amendment - Petition the government
129   Second Amendment - Militia; keep and bear arms
130   Third Amendment - Quartering of Soldiers
131   Fourth Amendment - Searches and seizures
132   Fifth Amendment - Grand jury
133   Fifth Amendment - Double jeopardy
134   Fifth Amendment - Self incrimination
135   Fifth Amendment - Due process
136   Fifth Amendment - Takings and just compensation
137   Sixth Amendment - Speedy and public trial
138   Sixth Amendment - Impartial jury
139   Sixth Amendment - Notification of charges
140   Sixth Amendment - Confrontation of witnesses
141   Sixth Amendment - Compulsory process
142   Sixth Amendment - Assistance of counsel
143   Seventh Amendment - Trial by jury, common law
144   Seventh Amendment - Integrity of jury findings
145   Eighth Amendment - No excessive bail or fines
146   Eighth Amendment - Cruel and unusual punishment
147   Ninth Amendment - Rights of the people
148   Tenth Amendment - States' rights
149   Eleventh Amendment - Sovereign immunity
150   Twelfth Amendment - Electoral college
151   Thirteenth Amendment - Involuntary servitude
152   Fourteenth Amendment - Definition of citizenship
153   Fourteenth Amendment - Privileges and immunities
154   Fourteenth Amendment - Due process
155   Fourteenth Amendment - Equal protection
156   Fifteenth Amendment - Voting
157   Sixteenth Amendment - Income tax
```

Table A.5 (continued)

158 Seventeenth Amendment - Direct election of senators
159 Nineteenth Amendment - Woman's suffrage
160 Twentieth Amendment - Lame ducks
161 Twenty-first Amendment - Repeal of Prohibition: state regulation of alcoholic beverages
162 Twenty-second Amendment - Limitation of terms of executive
163 Twenty-fourth Amendment - Abolition of poll tax
164 Twenty-fifth Amendment - Executive removal and succession
165 Twenty-sixth Amendment - 18 year old vote

The 200 Series: State Constitution
200 - 265 State constitutional analogues to federal constitutional provisions (Example: 225 state equal protection guarantee; 202 qualifications, elections of state legislators).
266 Specific due process guarantees - jury instructions
267 Specific due process guarantees - right to testify on one's behalf
268 Specific due process guarantees - right to appeal
269 Specific due process guarantees - ground for reversal of trial court
270 Specific due process guarantees - guarantee for habeas corpus
271 Regulation of public corporations
272 Property, water and mineral rights
273 Taxes, debts and finance
274 Home rule guarantee
275 Classifications of counties and cities
276 Prohibition against special legislation
277 Standards for judicial conduct at trials
278 Specific right to privacy
279 Regulation of alcoholic beverages
280 Status of the state universities
281 Statement of general police power
282 Educational guarantees
283 Requirement of germaneness
284 Status of the Public Service Commission
285 Guarantee of secret ballot

The 300 Series: State Statutes
300 Regulation of the Bar; lower state judiciary
301 Financial - taxes, finances, debts, appropriations, budget
302 Inheritance - wills, estates, probate
303 Government - elections, employees, municipalities
304 Education - teachers, school boards, schools
305 Domestic - marriage, divorce, custody, adoptions, age of majority
306 Motor vehicles
307 Property - zoning, eminent domain, rent control, property
308 Legal - "long arm," common law adoption, tort claims, extradition
309 Commercial - leases, investments, real estate transactions, insurance, sales, corporations
310 Workers - workmen's compensation, unemployment, retirement, collective bargaining
311 Administrative - hearings, appeals, appointment, rule-making, licenses
312 Criminal Procedure - general due process
313 Criminal Procedure - juries, grand juries; jury instructions
314 Criminal Procedure - jurisdiction of courts
315 Criminal Procedure - sentences
316 Criminal Procedure - witnesses; testimony
317 Criminal Procedure - evidence
318 Criminal Procedure - arrests; pre-trial procedure
319 Criminal Procedure - speedy trial
320 Criminal Procedure - bail; fines
321 Criminal Procedure - parole; probation
322 Criminal Procedure - appeals; post-conviction

Table A.5 (continued)

```
323    Criminal Procedure - juvenile justice
324    Criminal Procedure - pleas; plea bargaining
325    Criminal Procedure - searches and seizures
326    Criminal Procedure - exclusionary rule
237    Criminal Procedure - confessions
328    Criminal Procedure - assistance of counsel
329    Criminal Procedure - definition of crimes
330    Criminal Procedure - statute of limitations
331    Civil Procedure - statute of limitations
332    Civil Procedure - estoppel
333    Civil Procedure - appeals
334    Civil Procedure - settlements; directed verdicts
335    Civil Procedure - evidence
336    Civil Procedure - witnesses; testimony; depositions
337    Civil Procedure - declaratory judgments
338    Civil Procedure - damages; remedies
339    Civil Procedure - injunctions
340    Civil Procedure - commitment
341    Civil Procedure - jurisdiction
342    Civil Procedure - juries
343    Civil Procedure - definitions
344    Criminal Procedure - venue
345    Criminal Procedure - discovery
346    Civil Procedure - attorneys
347    Criminal Procedure - reversible errors; errors
348    Criminal Procedure - indictments
349    Civil Procedure - standing; class actions
350    Civil Procedure - discovery; pleadings
351    Civil Procedure - advisory opinions
352    Criminal Procedure - contempt
353    Criminal Procedure - role of district attorney
354    Criminal Procedure - habeas corpus
355    Criminal Procedure - commitment; competency
356    Environment - public health
357    Classifications - cities; counties
358    State Civil Rights Acts
359    Alcoholic Beverages
360    Morality - pornography; gambling
361    Non-Motor Vehicle Safety

The 400 Series: Common Law
400    Estoppel
401    Standards of proof
402    Burden of proof
403    res judicata
404    Interspousal immunity
405    Privileged communications
406    Retroactivity of decisions
407    Review of decisions; errors
408    Witnesses; testimony
409    Breach of confidence
410    Property; water and mineral rights; land; boundaries
411    Torts; negligence; liability; res ipsa locquitor
412    Contracts
413    Insanity; M'Naughton Rule
414    Domestic law; divorce; custody
415    Writs - habeas corpus; corum nobis
416    Resolution of the conflict of laws
417    Traditional role of grand juries
418    Common law definition of crimes
419    Rules of evidence
```

Table A.5 (continued)

420 Inheritance - wills; estates; codicils
421 Due process - hearings; plea bargaining; appeals
422 Equity; remedies
423 Misconduct of counsel; prejudice
424 Juries; jury instructions; jury questions
425 Defenses - duress; laches
426 Power of appointment
427 Directed verdicts; dismissals
428 Judicial - prosecutorial immunity
429 Objections; motions
430 Malicious prosecution
431 Mootness
432 Damages

The 500 Series: Federal Statutes
500 Federal Rules of Civil Procedure
501 U.S. Civil Rights Acts
502 Veterans
503 Fish and Wildlife
504 Extradition
505 Environmental Protection
506 Farmers Home Administration
507 Aid for Families with Dependent Children
508 Fair Labor Standards Act
509 Federal Communications Act
510 Federal Home Loan and Bank Board
511 Full Faith and Credit Act
512 Customs and Immigration
513 Interstate Commerce Act

Table A.6 En Banc State Statutory Cases

Variable	Arizona n	Arizona %	California n	California %	Kentucky n	Kentucky %	Michigan n	Michigan %	Nebraska n	Nebraska %	New Jersey n	New Jersey %	Significance[1]
Reverses Lower Court Decision	45	35.7	50	51.5	49	45.8	46	54.1	31	16.9	27	45.0	0.000
Unanimous Decisions	131	86.8	90	70.3	114	90.5	42	46.7	157	81.8	52	61.9	0.000
Full Dissenting Opinions Filed	9	6.0	24	18.8	8	6.3	30	33.3	18	9.4	17	20.2	0.000
Concurring Opinions Filed	9	6.0	9	7.0	2	1.6	17	18.9	7	3.6	13	15.5	0.000
Independent and Adequate State Grounds	78	51.7	92	71.9	107	84.9	70	77.8	149	77.6	62	73.8	0.000
Cases Decided Without Dissent	140	92.7	105	82.0	119	94.4	59	65.6	174	90.6	66	78.6	0.000
Judicial Activism Score													
(Least) 0	51	33.8	17	13.3	13	10.3	10	11.1	23	12.0	10	11.9	
1	64	42.4	69	53.9	98	77.8	50	55.6	133	69.3	48	57.1	
2	15	9.9	7	5.5	8	6.3	9	10.0	13	6.8	10	11.9	
3	12	7.9	16	12.5	4	3.2	10	11.1	13	6.8	4	4.8	0.000*
4	8	5.1	14	10.9	3	2.4	8	8.9	10	5.2	5	6.0	
5	1	0.7	1	0.8	0	0.0	2	2.2	0	0.0	5	6.0	
6	0	0.0	1	0.8	0	0.0	1	1.1	0	0.0	1	1.2	
(Most) 7	0	0.0	3	2.3	0	0.0	0	0.0	0	0.0	1	1.2	
Mean	1.1		1.71		1.10		1.62		1.24		1.64		
	n=151		n=128		n=126		n=90		n=192		n=84		Total N=771

[1] Significance levels marked by an asterisk should be treated with caution due to expected cell frequencies of five or less in the calculation of the chi-square value.

Table A.7 En Banc Common-Law Cases

Variable	Arizona		California		Kentucky		Michigan		Nebraska		New Jersey		Significance[1]
	n	%	n	%	n	%	n	%	n	%	n	%	
Reverses Lower Court Decision	4	20.0	12	42.9	33	61.1	26	63.4	15	12.7	14	50.0	0.000
Unanimous Decisions	21	87.5	26	66.7	47	81.0	22	52.4	97	80.2	20	60.6	0.001
Full Dissenting Opinions Filed	2	8.3	7	17.9	6	10.3	13	31.0	11	9.1	6	18.2	0.013*
Concurring Opinions Filed	1	4.2	2	5.1	1	1.7	7	16.7	2	1.7	6	18.2	0.000*
Independent and Adequate State Grounds	11	45.8	36	92.3	57	98.3	35	83.3	108	89.3	26	78.8	0.000*
Cases Decided Without Dissent	22	97.1	32	82.1	51	87.9	29	69.0	110	90.9	26	78.8	0.014*
Judicial Activism Score													
(Least) 0	5	20.8	1	2.6	1	1.7	3	7.1	9	7.4	6	18.2	0.000*
1	7	29.2	16	41.0	40	69.0	22	52.4	74	61.2	12	36.4	
2	3	12.5	4	10.3	7	12.1	5	11.9	13	10.7	4	12.1	
3	7	29.2	6	15.4	3	5.2	6	14.3	11	9.1	3	9.1	
4	2	8.3	6	15.4	6	10.3	6	14.3	14	11.6	5	15.2	
5	0	0.0	2	5.1	0	0.0	0	0.0	0	0.0	0	0.0	
6	0	0.0	1	2.6	1	1.7	0	0.0	0	0.0	1	3.0	
(Most) 7	0	0.0	3	7.7	0	0.0	0	0.0	0	0.0	2	6.1	
Mean	1.75		2.64		1.60		1.76		1.13		2.09		
	n=24		n=39		n=58		n=42		n=121		n=33		Total N=317

[1] Significance levels marked by an asterisk should be treated with caution due to expected cell frequencies of five or less in the calculation of the chi-square value.

Table A.8 En Banc Criminal Cases

Variable	Arizona		California		Kentucky		Michigan		Nebraska		New Jersey		Significance[1]
	n	%	n	%	n	%	n	%	n	%	n	%	
Reverses Lower Court Decision	26	24.3	20	52.6	14	50.0	24	61.5	16	10.7	14	48.3	0.000
Unanimous Decisions	110	89.4	28	49.1	26	76.5	16	40.0	123	79.9	16	48.5	0.000
Full Dissenting Opinions Filed	6	4.9	20	35.1	5	14.7	13	32.5	19	12.3	12	36.4	0.000
Concurring Opinions Filed	5	4.1	8	14.0	2	5.9	7	17.5	5	3.2	6	18.2	0.001*
Independent and Adequate State Grounds	46	37.4	28	49.1	24	70.6	26	65.0	108	70.1	21	63.6	0.000
Cases Decided Without Dissent	115	93.5	37	64.9	28	82.4	24	60.0	137	89.0	20	60.6	0.000
Judicial Activism Score													
(Least) 0	58	47.2	22	38.6	8	23.5	6	15.0	31	20.1	6	18.2	0.000*
1	48	39.0	19	33.3	22	64.7	23	57.5	101	65.6	17	51.5	
2	9	7.3	3	5.3	2	5.9	5	12.5	7	4.5	3	9.1	
3	7	5.7	7	12.3	0	0.0	5	12.5	9	5.8	1	3.0	
4	1	0.8	2	3.5	2	5.9	1	2.5	6	3.9	3	9.1	
5	0	0.0	2	3.5	0	0.0	0	0.0	0	0.0	2	6.1	
6	0	0.0	2	3.5	0	0.0	0	0.0	0	0.0	0	0.0	
(Most) 7	0	0.0	0	0.0	0	0.0	0	0.0	0	0.0	1	3.0	
Mean	0.74		1.33		1.00		1.30		1.08		1.67		
	n=123		n=57		n=34		n=40		n=154		n=33		Total N=441

[1]Significance levels marked by an asterisk should be treated with caution due to expected cell frequencies of five or less in the calculation of the chi-square value.

Table A.9 En Banc Criminal Constitutional Cases

Variable	Arizona n	Arizona %	California n	California %	Kentucky n	Kentucky %	Michigan n	Michigan %	Nebraska n	Nebraska %	New Jersey n	New Jersey %	Significance[1]
Reverses Lower Court Decision	12	18.2	11	47.8	2	25.0	10	71.4	5	10.9	5	50.0	0.000*
Unanimous Decisions	66	90.4	15	42.9	9	90.0	2	14.3	29	61.7	3	25.0	0.000*
Full Dissenting Opinions Filed	2	2.7	14	40.0	0	0.0	8	57.1	12	25.5	6	50.0	0.000*
Concurring Opinions Filed	5	6.8	6	17.1	1	10.0	3	21.4	4	8.5	4	33.3	ns
Independent and Adequate State Grounds	3	4.1	7	20.0	0	0.0	2	14.3	2	4.3	1	8.3	0.050*
Cases Decided Without Dissent	71	97.3	21	60.0	10	100.0	4	28.6	37	78.7	5	41.7	0.000*
Judicial Activism Score													
(Least) 0	51	69.9	21	60.0	8	80.0	4	28.6	31	66.0	6	50.0	0.001*
1	13	17.8	3	8.6	2	20.0	4	28.6	9	19.1	0	0.0	
2	4	5.5	2	5.7	0	0.0	3	21.4	2	4.3	1	8.3	
3	4	5.5	4	11.4	0	0.0	3	21.4	5	10.6	1	8.3	
4	1	1.4	1	2.9	0	0.0	0	0.0	0	0.0	2	16.7	
5	0	0.0	2	5.7	0	0.0	0	0.0	0	0.0	1	8.3	
6	0	0.0	2	5.7	0	0.0	0	0.0	0	0.0	0	0.0	
(Most) 7	0	0.0	0	0.0	0	0.0	0	0.0	0	0.0	1	8.3	
Mean	0.51		1.29		0.20		1.36		0.60		2.08		
	n=73		n=35		n=10		n=14		n=47		n=12		Total N=191

[1] Significance levels marked by an asterisk should be treated with caution due to expected cell frequencies of five or less in the calculation of the chi-square value.

Table A.10 En Banc Constitutional Cases

Variable	Arizona		California		Kentucky		Michigan		Nebraska		New Jersey		Significance[1]
	n	%	n	%	n	%	n	%	n	%	n	%	
Reverses Lower Court Decision	18	24.0	23	59.0	9	42.9	18	64.3	11	18.3	11	50.0	0.000
Unanimous Decisions	79	90.8	38	57.6	23	95.8	9	26.5	42	65.6	10	34.5	0.000
Full Dissenting Opinions Filed	2	2.3	18	27.3	0	0.0	15	44.1	14	21.9	10	34.5	0.000*
Concurring Opinions Filed	6	6.9	10	15.2	1	4.2	7	20.6	5	7.8	9	31.0	0.005*
Independent and Adequate State Grounds	8	9.2	15	22.7	4	16.7	14	41.2	8	12.5	4	13.8	0.001*
Cases Decided Without Dissent	85	97.7	48	72.7	24	100.0	17	50.0	51	79.7	17	58.6	0.000*
Judicial Activism Score (Least) 0	56	64.4	29	43.9	13	54.2	10	29.4	36	56.3	13	44.8	
1	18	20.7	12	18.2	10	41.7	13	38.2	15	23.4	3	10.3	
2	6	6.9	5	7.6	0	0.0	5	14.7	5	7.8	3	10.3	
3	5	5.7	9	13.6	1	4.2	4	11.8	7	10.9	3	10.3	0.000*
4	2	2.3	5	7.6	0	0.0	0	0.0	1	1.6	2	6.9	
5	0	0.0	2	3.0	0	0.0	1	2.9	0	0.0	4	13.8	
6	0	0.0	4	6.1	0	0.0	1	2.9	0	0.0	0	0.0	
(Most) 7	0	0.0	0	0.0	0	0.0	0	0.0	0	0.0	1	3.4	
Mean	0.61		1.56		0.54		1.35		0.78		1.83		
Criminal Cases	73	83.9	35	53.0	10	41.7	14	41.2	47	73.4	12	41.4	0.000
	n=87		n=66		n=24		n=34		n=64		n=29		Total N=304

[1] Significance levels marked by an asterisk should be treated with caution due to expected cell frequencies of five or less in the calculation of the chi-square value.

Bibliography

Adamany, David W. 1969. Party Variable in Judges' Voting: Conceptual Notes and a Case Study. *American Political Science Review*, 63:57–72.
Adamany, David W., and Philip DuBois. 1976. Electing State Judges. *Wisconsin Law Review*, 3:371–78.
Atkins, Burton M., and Henry R. Glick. 1976. Environmental and Structural Variables as Determinants of Issues in State Courts of Last Resort. *American Political Science Review*, 20:97–115.
———. 1974. Formal Judicial Recruitment and State Supreme Court Decisions. *American Politics Quarterly*, 2:427–49.
Barber, Kathleen. 1971. Ohio Elections—Nonpartisan Premises with Partisan Results. *Ohio State Law Journal*, 32:762–89.
Becker, Theodore L., and Malcolm M. Feeley, eds. 1973. *The Impact of Supreme Court Decisions*. New York: Oxford University Press.
Beiser, Edward N. 1974. The Rhode Island Supreme Court: A Well-Integrated Political System. *Law and Society Review*, 8:167–86.
Blalock, Herbert M., Jr. 1972. *Social Statistics*, 2d ed. New York: McGraw-Hill.
Borowiec, Walter A. 1976. Pathways to the Top: The Political Careers of State Supreme Court Justices. *North Carolina Central Law Journal*, 7:280–85.
Brennan, William J. 1977. State Constitutions and the Protection of Individual Rights. *Harvard Law Review*, 90:489–504.
Cameron, James Duke. 1977. The Place for Judicial Activism on the Part of a State's Highest Court. *Hastings Constitutional Law Quarterly*, 4:279–93.
Canon, Bradley C. 1972. The Impact of Formal Selection Processes on the Characteristics of Judges—Reconsidered. *Law and Society Review*, 6:579–93.

Chaffey, Douglas C. 1970. The Institutionalization of State Legislatures: A Comparative Study. *Western Political Quarterly*, 23:180–96.

Davies, Thomas J. 1982. State Intermediate Appellate Courts in the Legal Policy Process: A Case Study of Criminal Appeals. A paper presented to the 1982 Annual Meeting of the Law and Society Association, Toronto, Canada, June 3–6.

DuBois, Philip L. 1980. *From Ballot to Bench: Judicial Elections and the Quest for Accountability*. Austin: University of Texas Press.

———. 1979. The Significance of Voting Cues in State Supreme Court Elections. *Law and Society Review*, 13:757–79.

———. 1979. Voter Turnout in State Judicial Elections: An Analysis of the Tail on the Electoral Kite. *Journal of Politics*, 41:865–87.

Elazar, Daniel J. 1970. *Cities of the Prairie: The Metropolitan Frontier and American Politics*. New York: Basic Books, Inc.

———. 1966. *American Federalism: A View from the States*. New York: Thomas Y. Crowell.

Fenno, Richard F., Jr. 1973. *Congressmen in Committees*. Boston: Little, Brown and Co.

Friedelbaum, Stanley H. 1982. Independent State Grounds: Contemporary Invitations to Judicial Activism. In Mary Cornelia Porter and G. Alan Tarr, eds. *State Supreme Courts: Policymakers in the Federal System*. Westport, Conn.: Greenwood Press.

Glick, Henry R. 1971. *Supreme Courts in State Politics*. New York: Basic Books, Inc.

Glick, Henry R., and Kenneth N. Vines. 1973. *State Court Systems*. Englewood Cliffs, N.J.: Prentice-Hall, Inc.

———. 1969. Law-Making in the State Judiciary: A Comparative Study of the Judicial Role in Four States. *Polity*. 2:142–59.

Goldman, Sheldon. 1975. Voting Behavior on the United States Courts of Appeals Revisited. *American Political Science Review*, 69:491–506.

———. 1965. Characteristics of Eisenhower and Kennedy Appointees to the Lower Federal Courts. *Western Political Quarterly*, 18:755–62.

Herndon, James. 1962. Appointment as a Means of Initial Accession to Elective State Courts of Last Resort. *North Dakota Law Review*, 38:60–73.

Horowitz, Donald L. 1977. *The Courts and Social Policy*. Washington, D.C.: The Brookings Institution.

Jacob, Herbert. 1980. *Crime and Justice in Urban America*. Englewood Cliffs, N.J.: Prentice-Hall, Inc.

———. 1964. The Effect of Institutional Differences in the Recruitment Process: The Case of State Judges. *Journal of Public Law*, 13:104–19.

Kagan, Robert A., Bliss Cartwright, Lawrence M. Friedman and Stanton

Bibliography

Wheeler. 1978. The Evolution of State Supreme Courts. *Michigan Law Review*, 76:961–1005.

Jaros, Dean, and Bradley C. Canon. 1971. Dissent of State Supreme Courts: The Differential Significance of Characteristics of Judges. *Midwest Journal of Political Science*, 15:322–46.

Kim, Jae-On, and Charles W. Mueller. 1979. Introduction to Factor Analysis. Sage University Paper Series on Quantitative Applications in the Social Sciences, 07–013. Beverly Hills: Sage Publications.

———. 1978b. Factor Analysis: Statistical Methods and Practical Issues. Sage University Paper Series on Quantitative Applications in the Social Sciences, 07–014. Beverly Hills: Sage Publications.

Kluger, Richard. 1975. *Simple Justice: The History of Brown v. Board of Education and Black America's Struggle for Equality*. New York: Vintage Books.

Landinsky, Jack, and Allan Silver. 1967. Popular Democracy and Judicial Independence: Electorate and Elite Reactions to Two Wisconsin Supreme Court Elections. *Wisconsin Law Review*, 1967:128–69.

McConkie, Stanford S. 1976. Decision-Making in the State Supreme Courts. *Judicature*, 59:337–43.

Murphy, Walter F. 1964. *Elements of Judicial Strategy*. Chicago: University of Chicago Press.

Nagel, Stuart. 1962. Ethnic Affiliations and Judicial Propensities. *Journal of Politics*, 24:92–110.

Neuborne, Burt. 1977. The Myth of Parity. *Harvard Law Review*, 90:1105–1131.

Note. 1977. The New Federalism: Toward a Principled Interpretation of the State Constitution. *Stanford Law Review*, 29:297–321.

Perrow, Charles. 1979. *Complex Organizations: A Critical Essay*, 2d ed. Glenview, Ill.: Scott, Foresman and Company.

Polsby, Nelson W. 1968. The Institutionalization of the U.S. House of Representatives. *American Political Science Review*, 62:144–68.

Porter, Mary Cornelia. 1978. State Supreme Courts and the Legacy of the Warren Court: Some Old Inquiries for a New Situation. *Publius*, 1978:55–74.

Powell, Lee, ed. 1980. *Court Reform in Seven States*. National Center for State Courts: Publication No. 50054.

Romans, Neil T. 1974. Of State Supreme Courts in Judicial Policy-Making: Escobedo, Miranda, and the Use of Judicial Impact Analysis. *Western Political Quarterly*, 27:38–59.

Sarat, Austin. 1977. Studying American Legal Culture: An Assessment of Survey Evidence. *Law and Society Review*, 11:427–88.

Schmidhauser, John R. 1979. *Judges and Justices: The Federal Appellate Judiciary*. Boston: Little, Brown and Co.

Schmidhauser, John R. 1959. The Justices of the Supreme Court: A Collective Portrait. *Midwest Journal of Political Science*, 3:1–57.

Scott, Richard W. 1981. *Organizations: Rational, Natural and Open Systems*. Englewood Cliffs, N.J.: Prentice-Hall, Inc.

Sheldon, Charles H. 1974. *The American Judicial Process: Models and Approaches*. New York: Dodd, Mead and Co.

Sickels, Robert J. 1965. The Illusion of Judicial Consensus in Zoning Decisions on the Maryland Court of Appeals. *American Political Science Review*, 59:100–04.

Tarr, G. Alan. 1982. State Supreme Courts and the U.S. Supreme Court: The Problem of Compliance. In Mary Cornelia Porter and G. Alan Tarr, eds. *State Supreme Courts: Policymakers in the Federal System*. Westport, Conn.: Greenwood Press.

Tobin, Robert W., and Richard B. Hoffman. 1979. *The Administrative Role of Chief Justices and Supreme Courts*. National Center for State Courts: Publication No. 10046.

Ulmer, Sidney S. 1970. Dissent Behavior and the Social Backgrounds of Supreme Court Justices. *Journal of Politics*, 32:375–84.

———. 1966. Politics and Procedure in the Michigan Supreme Court. *Southwestern Social Science Quarterly*, 46:375–84.

———. 1964. The Political Party Variable in the Michigan Supreme Court. *Journal of Public Law*, 11:352–62.

Vines, Kenneth N. 1969. The Judicial Role in the American States: An Exploration. In Joel Grossman and Joseph Tannehaus, eds. *Frontiers of Judicial Research*. New York: John Wiley.

———. 1964. Federal District Judges and Race Relations Cases in the South. *Southern Journal of Politics*, 26:337–57.

Vines, Kenneth N., and Herbert Jacob. 1971. State Courts. In Herbert Jacob and Kenneth N. Vines, eds. *Politics in the American States: A Comparative Analysis*, 2d ed. Boston: Little, Brown and Co.

Watson, Richard A., and Rondal G. Downing. 1969. *The Politics of the Bench and the Bar: Judicial Selection under the Missouri Nonpartisan Court Plan*. New York: John Wiley and Sons, Inc.

Winters, Glenn R., and Robert E. Allard. 1965. Judicial Selection and Tenure in the United States. In Harry W. Jones, ed. *The Courts, the Public and the Law Explosion*. Englewood Cliffs, N.J.: Prentice-Hall, Inc.

Wold, John T. 1974. Political Orientation, Social Backgrounds and Role Perceptions of State Supreme Court Judges. *Western Political Quarterly*, 27:239–48.

Index to Cases

Advisory Opinion re Constitutionality of 1974 P.A. 242, 99
Barron v. Mayor and City Council of Baltimore, 23
Bonneville, People v., 93
Botsch v. Riesdorf, 110
Braitman v. Overlook Terrace, 110
Brisendine, People v., 91, 92
Burnette v. Borough of New Milford, 110
Burnick, People v., 93
City of Los Angeles v. City of San Fernando, 91, 93
Crampton v. Department of State, 99
Darby, United States v., 1
Dearborn Firefighters Union Local No. 412 I.A.F.F.N. v. City of Dearborn, 109
Department of Natural Resources and Environmental Protection v. No. 8 Limited of Virginia, 96
Dupuy v. Superior Court, 93
Escobedo v. Illinois, 20
Feagley, People v., 93
Fuentes v. Shevlin, 109
Garcia v. San Antonio Metropolitan Transit Authority, 23
Gertsch v. Gerber, 110
Goldberg, State v., 88
Gould v. Gruble, 93
Hackensack Meadowlands v. Municipal Landfill Authority, 107
Heilman v. Snyder, 109
Holmberg, State v., 109
Hutton Park Gardens v. West Orange Town Council, 110
Klopping v. City of Whittier, 110

Krol, State v., 107, 110
Kube v. Kube, 109
Li v. Yellow Cab Co., 93
Longnecker v. Noordyk-Mooney, Inc., 99
Longwill, People v., 109
Lubash v. Langmeier, 110
Manistee Bank and Trust Co. v. McGowan, 99
Meyer v. State Farm Mutual Auto Insurance Co., 109
Miranda v. Arizona, 20
National League of Cities v. Usery, 2, 23
National Land and Investment Co. v. Eastown Board of Adjustment, 109
Neal v. Hunt, 88
Nebraska Press Association v. Stuart, 109
Nebraska Public Service Commission v. Chicago and N.W. Transportation Co., 102
Nickola v. Grand Blanc Township, 109
Norman, People v., 109
Parham v. Commonwealth, 96
Philadelphia v. New Jersey, 110
Request for Advisory Opinion of 1975 P.A. 227, 109
Request for Advisory Opinion on Constitutionality of 1975 P.A. 195, 196, 109
Richards v. Omaha Public Schools, 103
Robinson v. Cahill, 106, 107, 110
Rodriguez, In re, 91
Royal Indemnity Co. v. Aetna Casualty and Surety Co., 103
Sabo v. Monroe Township, 109
Sherdon v. Dann, 110
Simants, State v., 102
Smookler v. Wheatfield Township, 109
Snaidach v. Family Finance Corp., 109
South Burlington County N.A.A.C.P. v. Township of Mount Laurel, 108, 110
State ex rel. Meyer v. American Community Stores Corp., 110
Stephens v. Commonwealth, 96
Stone v. Powell, 2
Svitak, State v., 109
Terry v. Ohio, 91
Thorton v. Carson, 89
Troy Hills Village v. Parsippany-Troy Hills Township Council, 110
Washington Market Enterprises v. Trenton, 110
Williams v. Nebraska City Airport Authority, 110
Wingo, People v., 91

Subject Index

Adamany, David W., 24 n.11, 75
Administrative Law and Procedure, 4, 93, 99, 114-15
Advisory Opinions, 99
Allard, Robert E., 56, 58
American Bar Association: and Missouri Plan, 39, 58; and model court system, 38, 89, 94, 113
The American Bench, 49
Appointment of Judges, 40, 50, 55, 89. *See also* Judicial Recruitment Plans
Atkins, Burton M., 9, 15, 17, 37-40, 57, 68, 85

Barber, Kathleen, 24 n.11
Becker, Theodore L., 23 n.2
Beiser, Edward N., 19-20
Bill of Rights, 22, 63, 100, 117; nationalization of, 2, 23 n.4
Blalock, Herbert M., 64 n.5
Borowiec, Walter A., 18
Brennen, William, 2-3, 37, 81
Burger, Warren, 2-3, 66, 112
Burger Court, 78, 80, 82, 89-91, 112

Cameron, James Duke, 115
Canon, Bradley C., 17-18, 39-40, 57, 75, 85

Canon of Judicial Ethics, 63
Cartwright, Bliss, 9
Cases: classification of, 35-38, 67-68; constitutional, 76, 83-84, 89, 95-105, 111; statutory/regulatory, 78, 92, 95-98, 105, 107, 110 n.23
Chaffey, Douglas C., 64 n.1
Chief Justices, 40-41, 54-55
Citation of Law Review and Periodicals: in "good" courts, 5-6; in six state comparison, 67, 93, 99, 102, 106, 115
Civil Liberties, 105; stricter standards for protection of, 22, 86 n.6
Coleman, Mary Stallings, 77, 98
Commitment, Civil or Criminal, 107
Common Law, 68, 93, 95, 103, 105; and judicial activism, 77-79
Compensable Takings, 104, 108
Congress: House of Representatives, 76-77, 116; institutionalization in, 14
Congressional committees, 76-77, 116
Court systems: administration and supervision of, 14, 19, 40-41, 105, 108, 110 n.23, 114-15; institutional characteristics of, 15, 19,

Subject Index

Court systems (*Continued*) 21, 25-47, 65, 87-109; organization of, 10, 27-46, 60-61
Criminal Justice: in Arizona, 79, 82, 88, 112; in California, 82, 91-92; and environmental variables, 37; and judicial activism, 79-83, 112; in Kentucky, 82, 97-98; in Moralistic culture, 11; in Nebraska, 82, 101-102; in New Jersey, 79, 82, 107; in Texas, 29; and U.S. Supreme Court, 2
Cruel and Unusual Punishment, 91

Davies, Thomas J., 81-82, 85
Decision-making: attitudes in, 15-17, 49; institutional characteristics and, 14, 25, 39; institutionalization and, 14; judicial tenure and, 59; judicial recruitment and, 16-17, 39-40; norms in, 76-77, 85, 115-16; role perception in, 17-20; in state supreme courts, 3-4, 14, 76-77, 86 n.4; in U.S. House of Representatives, 77; in U.S. Supreme Court, 1, 3
Democratic Party, 56-58, 75, 97, 100
Desegregation, 2, 16
Dissent: in California, 82; contributing factors in, 75, 85; and decision-making norms, 76-77, 115; judicial background and, 16-17, 22, 75; in Kentucky, 76; in Michigan, 75-76, 82, 97, 100, 106, 112-13; in Nebraska, 84, 101; in New Jersey, 82, 105; rates of, 21-22, 66, 72-85, 111-13
Downing, Rondal G., 15, 46 n.8, 58
DuBois, Philip, 24 n.11, 46 n.8

Due Process, 2, 23 n.4, 37, 66, 89, 92-93, 108

Eastonian Systems Model, 37-38
Economic Development: in Michigan, 97, 112
Economic Regulation, 117
Eighth Amendment, 80
Elazar, Daniel J., 6-11, 24 n.7, 26-27, 43, 46 nn.4, 5, 73-74, 87-104, 111-12
Election Law, 93
Englander, Arthur, 39, 47 n.10
Environmental Protection, 107
Equal Protection, 2, 37, 83, 92-93, 99, 103

Factor Analysis, 42
Fair Labor Standards Act, 100
Federal Communications Commission, 103
Federalism. *See* Judicial Federalism
Federal Judiciary Act of 1789, 102
Feeley, Malcolm M., 23 n.2
Fenno, Richard F., Jr., 76, 85, 115
Fifth Amendment, 66, 80, 83, 96, 98
First Amendment, 83, 92-93, 99
Fourteenth Amendment, 23, 89, 93
Fourth Amendment, 66, 78, 80, 83, 88, 91, 96, 98, 103
Free Press-Fair Trial, 102
Friedelbaum, Stanley H., 70
Friedman, Lawrence M., 9

Glick, Henry R., 9, 15, 17, 19, 37-40, 57, 68, 85, 105
Goldman, Sheldon, 16
Guest Passenger Statutes: automobile, 67, 99, 103; aviation, 99

Habeas Corpus, 24 n.6
Hand, Learned, 13

Subject Index

Herndon, James, 24n.10
Hobbes, Thomas, 10
Hoffman, Richard B., 24n.8, 47 n.11
Horowitz, Donald L., 23 n.3
Hughes, Justice, 106-108

Independent and Adequate State Grounds, 3-6, 20, 63, 70-71, 78-84, 86 n.6, 89, 96, 111-12, 117; operational definition of, 5-6
Institutionalization: defined, 14, 18; judicial activism and, 21; judicial recruitment and, 18-19, 49, 62-63, 114; in organizations, 18-19, 25 n.1, 46, 114; in state courts, 14-15, 54; in state legislature, 64 n.1
Interim Appointment of Judges, 17, 24 n.10, 55, 57-58, 114, 129
Intermediate Appellate Courts: in Arkansas, 28-29; in Arizona, 73, 89, 117; in California, 73, 81, 91-92; creation of, 13, 37; dissent and reversal rates and, 22, 73-75, 82-85, 115; in Kentucky, 73, 82, 94, 96, 117; and merit element, 30, 34, 91; in Nebraska, 73, 82, 102-104, 117; in New Jersey, 73, 108; political culture and, 31; as reform, 116-17; relationship with state supreme courts, 4, 14-15, 25, 28, 37, 39-42, 62, 113, 117; as variable, 38-41, 85
Internal Unity, 87-88, 111-13; in Arizona, 74, 88, 90, 94, 111; in California, 90-91; dissent and reversals and, 22, 73-75, 85; in Kentucky, 74, 90, 94; in Michigan, 94, 97, 99-100, 111-112; in Nebraska, 90, 100, 111; in New Jersey, 74, 104, 111; and socioeconomic diversity, 6-8

Jacksonian Democracy, 34
Jacob, Herbert, 8, 38, 40
Jaros, Dean, 17, 75, 85
Judges and Justices: attitudes of, 15-16, 49; career patterns of, 49-51, 56-57, 62-63; "maverick", 22, 75, 84-85; methods of removal from office of, 20; political and social backgrounds of, 12, 16-18, 50-51, 56-57, 62-63, 85, 114; qualifications for office of, 51; role perceptions of, 17, 19-20, 61; salaries of, 3, 27-28, 31, 41-42, 89, 92-97, 101, 105, 108; support staff for, 3, 31-32, 41-42, 89, 92-95, 105, 108
Judicial Activism: in Arizona, 77-82, 88-89; in California, 21, 77-80, 83, 89-90, 93; in criminal cases, 79-80; definition of, 5-6; and judicial administration, 115, and judicial independence, 13, in Kentucky, 77-78, 81; in Michigan, 78-81, 83, 97; in Nebraska, 77-78, 81, 83; in New Jersey, 19, 21, 78-83, 104, 108-109; recruitment and, 20-21; reversals/dissent and, 81; role perception and, 19-20; state comparison and, 69-93, 111, 117; variables/norms in, 115
Judicial Backgrounds: chief justices' and associates' compared, 54-55; and court classification, 60-61; decision-making and, 1, 15-17, 39-40; dissent and, 16-17, 75; formal recruitment and, 15-17, 56-57, 60-63, 114, 122; and geographic region, 31-36, 39, 43, 56, 114; and interim appointee, 57-58; and political culture, 10-11, 31-34,

Judicial Backgrounds (*Continued*) 43; similarity of, 50; and term of office, 59-60, 114, 122; and voting behavior, 16-17. *See also* Judges and Justices
Judicial Elections, 10, 21, 28, 39, 55, 64 n.2, 95, 113-114, 116; and campaigns, 63; low salience of, 17, 34, 63; in Michigan, 75, 97
Judicial Federalism, 35, 66-85, 116
Judicial Independence, 13, 41, 50, 71, 94, 114
Judicial Nominating Commission, 29-30
Judicial Professionalism Score, 38, 71, 89, 92, 95, 98, 101, 105
Judicial Qualifications Commissions, 30, 34-35, 43, 58, 89, 92, 95, 97, 101, 113
Judicial Recruitment: and court classification, 38-40, 42, 60-61; and court reform, 15; decision-making and, 16-17; institutionalization and, 62; judicial background and, 12, 16-18, 39, 50-57, 60-62; and merit selection, 10, 28-31, 34, 39, 43, 58-59, 63, 71, 92, 97, 114; Missouri Plan and, 28, 34, 38, 55; in New Jersey, 105; political culture and, 10-11, 31-34, 40, 43, 113; relationship with geographic region, 31-34, 36, 39, 43, 56-57, 59, 62; term of office and, 59-60
Judicial Recruitment Plans, 39-50, 55-57, 63, 91-92, 97, 113, 116; appointive, 20-21, 34, 40, 50, 55-57, 63, 89, 105, 116; and court classification, 39-40; elective plans, 10, 21, 34, 40, 50, 55-57, 116; mixed plans, 34, 40, 55-57; and region, 39, 56-57

Judicial Review: as reform, 117; reversal rates and, 73; in state supreme courts, 15, 67, 73, 78, 82-83, 89, 93, 99; and U.S. Supreme Court, 3
Judicial Role, 17, 19-20, 61
Judicial Tenure Commission, 97
Jury Instructions, 80

Kagan, Robert A., 9, 13, 35, 37, 68, 85, 86 n.1, 2
Kim, Jae-On, 41-42
Kluger, Richard, 86 n.4

Labor Law and Relations, 23 n.5, 100
Landinsky, Jack, 24 n.11
Landlord-Tenant Relations, 104
Legal Culture, 8
Legislative Election of Judges, 10, 28, 38, 55
Limited Jurisdiction Courts, 38
Litigation Rates: and political culture, 10-11
Locke, John, 10

McConkie, Stanford S., 46 n.3
McCown, Hale, 75, 84
Medical Malpractice, 96
Mentally Disordered Sex Offender Statute, 93
Merit Plan, 10, 29-30, 34, 39, 43, 50, 58-59. *See also* Missouri Plan
Michigan Employees Relation Commission, 99-100
Missouri Plan, 28, 34, 38-39, 50, 55, 101, 113
Mosk, Stanley, 91
Mueller, Charles W., 42
Murphy, Walter F., 86 n.4

Nagel, Stuart, 16
Nebraska Budget Act, 103

Subject Index

Negligence, 103
Neuborne, Burt, 3, 35, 39
Nixon Court, 66
Nonpartisan election: in California, 92; in Moralistic Culture, 10; in Michigan, 75, 97, 100; recruitment and, 17, 28, 31-34, 38, 55-56

Partisan Election, 10, 28, 34, 38-39, 55, 63
Pashman, Morris, 75, 110 n.28
Perrow, Charles, 24 n.9, 46 n.1
Police Power, 108; and takings, 96
Political Culture: in Arizona, 89, 94; in California, 91-92; defined, 6-12; dissent and 85; dominant, 46 n.4; geographic region and, 26-27, 31, 113; Individualistic, 10, 26, 31, 43, 91-95, 101, 105, 113; institutional characteristics of, 25, 31, 43, 113; judicial background and, 57; judicial recruitment and, 31-34, 40, 113-14; in Kentucky, 94-95, 113; in Michigan, 97; Moralistic, 10, 26, 31, 34-35, 43, 89, 91-92, 97, 101; in Nebraska, 101; in New Jersey, 94, 105; Traditionalistic, 11, 26, 31, 35, 43, 89, 94-95, 113
Polsby, Nelson, 13-14, 18, 49, 62, 64 n.1
Populist Movement, 34
Porter, Mary Cornelia, 5
Powell, Lee, 47 nn.9, 10, 109 n.4
Powell, Lewis F., Jr., 24 n.6
Precedents: use of sister state, 5-6, 66-67, 71, 84, 99, 102, 115
Property Disputes, 95
Public Policy, 1-2; in New Jersey, 106-108
Public Service Commission, 103

Rehnquist, William, 2, 23 n.5
Rent Control, 104, 108
Replevin Statutes, 89, 109 n.2
Republican Party, 54, 57-58, 75, 97, 100
Reversals: explanations of variation in rates of, 73-74; rates of, 21-22, 66, 71-78, 81-85, 111, 115
Romans, Neil T., 20
Roosevelt Court, 1
Rousseau, Jean-Jacques, 10

Sarat, Austin, 8
Schmidhauser, John R., 13, 15-16, 19, 71
School Finance, 106-107
Scott, Richard W., 46 n.1
Searches and Seizures, 78, 88, 91
Sentences: in Arizona, 88; in California, 91; review of, 73
Sheldon, Charles H., 23 n.1
Sickels, Robert J., 76, 115
Silver, Allan, 24 n.11
Sixth Amendment, 68, 80, 98
Spencer, Justice, 102
Stare Decisis, 11, 81
State Court Systems, 26, 46 n.2, 49, 65-66
State Regulatory Statutes: in Michigan, 98; in New Jersey, 105
State Supreme Court Classification System, 35-46, 60-61
Statutory Interpretation, 67, 95, 100
Supremacy Clause, 22-23, 86 n.6
Supreme Courts, state: in Alaska, 31, 47 n.15, 118; in Arkansas, 28, in Arizona, 26, 65-109, 111-12, 116, 118; in California, 3, 21, 28, 31, 65-109, 116-17; caseload effect on, 9, 35-37, 39, 62, 90, 102, 104; classification of, 35-39, 44-45, 67-68; in Connecticut, 28;

Supreme Courts (*Continued*)
in Delaware, 17, 28, 43; in Florida, 34, 39; and "good" performance, 3-5; in Hawaii, 28, 47 n.15; in Illinois, 97; indicator of performance for, 4, 6-7; institutional characteristics of, 13-15, 19, 25-47, 65-113; institutionalization in, 14, 18-19; judicial activism and, 5, 69-71; in Kentucky, 65-109, 113, 116-17; in Louisiana, 19; in Maine, 28; in Maryland, 17, 76; in Michigan, 65-118; in Mississippi, 3, 28; in Missouri, 43; model of performance for, 1-23, 65; in Nebraska, 65-109, 111, 117; in New Hampshire, 28, 59; in New Jersey, 3, 19, 21, 28, 59, 65-117; in New Mexico, 26; in New York, 3, 17, 21, 31, 97; in Oklahoma, 43, 49, 46 n.6; parity with federal courts, 2, 24 n.6; in Pennsylvania, 31; relationship with U.S. Supreme Court, 2, 20, 63, 89, 91, 117; responsibilities of, 89-90; in Rhode Island, 19-20, 27, 59; in South Carolina, 28; staff on, 31-32, 41-42, 89-95, 105, 108; in Texas, 28, 31, 46 n.6, 49; in Utah, 3, 31; in Virginia, 17, 28; work of, 69; in Wyoming, 31
Supreme Court, United States, 102; and Arizona Supreme Court, 89, 109 n.2, 112; and California Supreme Court, 91; conservatism of, 66, 82; policy-making and, 1; social background of, 15-16; and state supreme courts, 2-3, 8, 20, 63, 79, 82; unanimity in decisions, 86 n.4

Tarr, G. Alan, 117
Taxes and Taxation, 93
Tenth Amendment, 1-2, 23 n.4, 5
Tobin, Robert W., 24 n.8, 47 n.11
Trial Courts, 73-74, 81, 102

Ulmer, Sidney S., 16, 75

Vanderbilt, Arthur, 19, 105, 108
Variable: contextual, 25, 73, 85, 111, 113, 115; dependent, 37; environmental, 37, 85n.1; independent, 111; institutional, 25, 85, 111-15; structural, 38-39, 85 n.1
Vines, Kenneth N., 16, 19, 38, 105

Warrantless searches, 91
Warren Court, 2, 66
Waste Control Act, 107
Water Rights, 88, 91, 93, 111-12
Watson, Richard A., 15, 46n.8, 58
Wheeler, Stanton, 9
Who's Who, 49
Williams, G. Mennen, 77, 98
Winter, Glenn R., 56, 58
Wold, John T., 17
Workmen's Compensation, 78, 95, 97, 102

Zoning, 76, 95, 99, 105; exclusionary, 104, 108

About the Author

SUSAN P. FINO is Assistant Professor of Political Science at Wayne State University. She has also been selected as an alternate for the 1987–1988 National Judicial Fellowship.